Adolescent Abortion

Children and the Law

General Editors:
Gary B. Melton
Lois A. Weithorn

Consulting Editors:
Thomas Grisso
Gerald P. Koocher
Robert H. Mnookin
Walter J. Wadlington

Edited by Gary B. Melton

Adolescent Abortion

Psychological and Legal Issues

Report of the Interdivisional Committee
on Adolescent Abortion,
American Psychological Association

University of Nebraska Press
Lincoln and London

The paper in this book meets the minimum requirements
of American National Standard for
Information Sciences – Permanence of Paper for Printed
Library Materials, ANSI Z39.48-1984.

Library of Congress Cataloging in Publication Data
Main entry under title:
Adolescent abortion.
(Children and the law)
Includes index.
1. Abortion – Psychological aspects. 2. Pregnancy,
Adolescent – Psychological aspects. 3. Abortion
counseling. 4. Pregnant schoolgirls – Counseling of.
I. Melton, Gary B. II. American Psychological
Association. Interdivisional Committee on Adolescent
Abortion. III. Series. [DNLM: 1. Abortion, Induced –
in adolescence. 2. Abortion, Induced – psychology.
3. Child Advocacy. 4. Counseling – in adolescence.
5. Pregnancy in Adolescence. WS 462 A2385]
RG734.A35 1986 362.1'9888'088055 85-31812
ISBN 0-8032-3094-X (alk. paper)

CONTENTS

PREFACE

This monograph is the product of a committee sponsored by several divisions of the American Psychological Association (APA). The committee was charged with reviewing what is known and not known about psychological issues that have been central to the Supreme Court's analysis of adolescent abortion policy and with providing guidelines to psychologists involved in counseling minors about abortion or conducting research on the issue.

The committee was initiated by the Division of Child, Youth, and Family Services (Division 37) and cosponsored by Divisions 34 (Population and Environment), 35 (Psychology of Women), and 41 (American Psychology–Law Society). A summary of the committee's report, to be published in *American Psychologist*, has been endorsed by the executive committees of the sponsoring divisions and represents their policy. It has also been noted with favor by the APA Committee on Women in Psychology and the APA Committee for Protection of Human Participants in Research. The statement has not been considered by the APA Council of Representatives, however, and is therefore not the official policy of the organization as a whole.

Members of the Interdivisional Committee on Adolescent Abortion included Nancy E. Adler, Henry P. David, Jeanne Marecek, Gary B. Melton (chair), Roberta A. Morris, Nancy Felipe Russo, Elizabeth S. Scott, Lois A. Weithorn, and Kathleen Wells.

GARY B. MELTON AND ANITA J. PLINER

Adolescent Abortion: A Psycholegal Analysis

Few issues in our society are as emotion laden as the conditions under which abortion should be legally available. The issue is especially charged in regard to adolescents, because it raises the profound dilemma of the proper ordering of the interests of the adolescent, her family, and the state. The question is no less basic than whether adolescents are to be considered true persons entitled to privacy in personal decisions (see Melton, 1983c).

Beyond the profound moral and social issues involved in abortion generally and in parent-child-state relations generally, the sheer frequency of adolescent abortion makes it a social phenomenon worthy of careful policy analysis. In both absolute and relative terms, abortion is common among adolescents (see Russo, this volume, for a review). About 40% of the 1.1 million pregnancies of females under age 20 annually are terminated by induced abortions. Nearly one-third of all abortions are performed on females under age 20.

In addition to the general public interest in issues related to adolescent abortion, psychologists have special interest in the problem, for several resons. First, as we shall see, the Supreme Court has emphasized psychological factors in deciding cases on abortion by minors. Psychologists can assist courts and legislatures in evaluating the validity of psychological assumptions to determine whether any compelling basis exists for age-based regulation of women's access to abortion. Similarly, psychologists can evaluate legal procedures to ensure that these procedures enhance support for pregnant adolescents and do not add undue stress or create unintended negative effects.

Second, as clinicians or counselors in schools, mental health centers, and health care settings, psychologists often assist adolescent clients or other health professionals in making decisions about abortion. Few situations raise as many complex ethical and legal problems for psychologists who seek to provide the scientific basis for practice through study of pregnant adolescents' decisions or the effects of their decisions.

Third, and most generally, as scientists and professionals committed to promoting human welfare (American Psychological Association, 1981, Preamble), psychologists are dedicated to ensuring that adolescents and families faced with difficult decisions have access to services that will assist them in understanding the alternatives and dealing with their consequences. Psychologists are ethically bound to respect individual privacy and to protect the civil rights of their clients (APA, 1981, Principle 3c).

Clearly, policy on adolescent abortion is likely to have far-reaching significance, and psychological concerns have been central in the debate on the issue. In this chapter we present an overview of the law and psychology of adolescent abortion. The development of the law on the subject will be reviewed, with special attention to the psychological justifications for prevailing law. We will then examine what is known about the validity of these justifications. In view of both existing law and existing psychological knowledge, we conclude with recommendations for psychologists involved in counseling or research on adolescent abortion and for policymakers who wish to consider psychological knowledge in formulating policy on adolescent abortion.

THE DEVELOPMENT OF THE LAW

The question of the limits of minors' access to abortion is relatively recent in law. Indeed, less than 25 years ago, *any* woman who elected to terminate her pregnancy usually had to resort to illegal, unsanitary, and unsafe means. Abortion was frequently considered a criminal offense committed by the woman and the physician performing the procedure.

The Supreme Court cases leading to the legalization of abortion began in 1963 with *Griswold v. Connecticut,*[1] a landmark case in which a constitutional right to privacy was first recognized by the Supreme Court. In *Griswold,* the Court invalidated a Connecticut statute that made possession and use of contraceptives by married couples a criminal offense. Drawing from the "penumbras" of the Bill of Rights and the Fourteenth Amendment, the Court held that such regulation of procreation was a direct violation of the right to privacy in decisions about personal matters.

The *Griswold* holding was later expanded to encompass the woman's right not only to prevent but to terminate her pregnancy. In the famous 1973 case of *Roe v. Wade,*[2] the Court held that state regulation of a woman's access to abortion at all times during her pregnancy is impermissible. In finding unconstitutional a Texas statute that proscribed abortion unless it was performed to save the mother's life, the Court eliminated most restrictions on an adult woman's right to abortion. Subsequent to *Roe,* any limitation on the woman's fundamental right to abortion would have to be justified by a compelling state interest. In so holding, the Court in effect invalidated the abortion laws of 46 states (Mnookin, 1985).

The woman's right to abortion under *Roe* is not absolute. During the first trimester, the absence of a compelling state interest precludes the state's interference. Throughout this stage of pregnancy, the abortion decision rests solely with the woman in consultation with her physician. However, as the pregnancy advances and the state's interest in safeguarding the mother's life and protecting the potential life becomes compelling, this bilateral decision-making model becomes subject to state regulation.

Second-trimester abortions may be regulated by the state "to

---

1. 381 U.S. 479 (1965).
2. 410 U.S. 113 (1973).

the extent that the regulation is reasonably designed to further the preservation and protection of maternal health."[3] When the fetus becomes viable, a point in time defined as the 22nd week of pregnancy,[4] the state may go so far as to proscribe abortion to protect the potential life, unless the physician determines the abortion is necessary to preserve the life or health of the mother. This trimester approach to defining the extent to which a state may constitutionally curtail a woman's access to abortion has been reaffirmed in subsequent Supreme Court decisions.[5]

While the *Roe* Court clearly established the right of adult women to choose between abortion and childbirth, it did not address the degree to which this right applied to minors. Traditionally, minors have not been extended the same breadth of constitutional rights accorded to adults.[6] Indeed, it was not until 1967 that the Supreme Court made it clear that minors are "persons" within the meaning of the Bill of Rights and the Fourteenth Amendment.[7] A state's interests in protecting minors' welfare and promoting family integrity often provide adequate justification for state infringement of minors' constitutional rights. Recognizing these interests and the failure of the Court to address specifically the extent of minors' independent access to abortion, many legislatures responded to *Roe* by enacting legislation requiring parental involvement in pregnant minors' decisions about abortion. Unsurprisingly, the Supreme Court received ample opportunity to review several of the statutory schemes.

The Court first reviewed the constitutionality of the parental consent requirement in *Planned Parenthood of Central Missouri v. Danforth.*[8] The Missouri statute at issue in *Danforth* required the

3. *Id.* at 163.
4. *Id.* at 163.
5. *See, e.g.*, City of Akron v. Akron Center for Reproductive Health, 103 S.Ct. 2481, 2492–97 (1983).
6. *See, e.g.*, Parham v. J. R., 442 U.S. 584 (1979); McKeiver v. Pa., 403 U.S. 528 (1971); Ginsberg v. N.Y., 390 U.S. 629 (1968); Prince v. Mass., 321 U.S. 158 (1944).
7. *In re* Gault, 387 U.S. 1, 13 (1967).
8. 428 U.S. 52 (1976) (hereinafter cited as *Danforth*).

written consent of at least one parent for all first-trimester abortions performed on unmarried minors. This provision vested the minor's parent with a blanket authority to veto her abortion decision, a power the Court found to create an undue burden on the minor's access to abortion and, therefore, her constitutional right to privacy. Acknowledging this right, the Court proclaimed that "rights do not mature and come into being magically only when one attains the state defined age of majority."[9] At the same time, however, the Court made it clear that minors' access to abortion could be limited in ways that would be unconstitutional if applied to adults. The standard of scrutiny of state statutes regulating minor abortion was to be merely whether a *significant*—not *compelling*—state interest was furthered.[10] The Court also emphasized that its holding "does not suggest that every minor, regardless of age or maturity, may give effective consent for termination of her pregnancy."[11] Moreover, the holding itself was limited. Although providing an *absolute* veto power to parents was held to be unconstitutional, the Court left the door open to consideration of other statutory requirements for parental involvement in minors' abortion decisions.

The Court next considered the boundaries of mandated parental involvement in *Bellotti v. Baird*.[12] At issue was the constitutionality of a Massachusetts statute that required an unmarried pregnant minor to seek the consent of both parents before an abortion could be performed. If parental consent was denied, the minor could then seek judicial authorization for the abortion. Problems in the statute were twofold. First, the Massachusetts law vested an absolute veto power in a third party, in this case the minor's parents or a judge. A judge could overrule a minor's abortion decision even if she were found mature enough to give informed consent to the

9. *Id.* at 74.
10. *Id.* 75.
11. *Id.* 75.
12. 443 U.S. 622 (1979) (hereinafter cited as *Bellotti II*). The Supreme Court had previously considered *Bellotti* as a companion to *Danforth* and remanded it for interpretation of the statute in question by the Massachusetts Supreme Judicial Court, Bellotti v. Baird I, 428 U.S. 132 (1976).

procedure. Second, *all* minors seeking an abortion, regardless of their maturity, first had to seek parental consent. *Bellotti* made it clear that, by failing to allow minors to bypass parents in abortion decisions, Massachusetts had created an impermissible burden on minors' right to privacy.

The *Bellotti* plurality offered a blueprint for a judicial bypass statute that would withstand a constitutional challenge. The two-tier test outlined by the Court has since been adopted in several jurisdictions.[13] If a minor chooses to seek judicial approval (in lieu of parental consent) of an abortion, the judge must first determine if the minor is sufficiently mature to make a reasoned, informed decision. If so, the inquiry stops and the abortion must be granted. If, however, the judge finds that the minor is immature, a determination must be made whether an abortion would be in her best interests.

As the scope of the constitutional regulation of parental consent was refined, so too were the permissible limits of parental notification requirements. The first test of such a statute before the Supreme Court came in 1981 in *H. L. v. Matheson*.[14] In *Matheson*, the Court upheld a Utah statute that subjected physicians to criminal penalties if they failed to notify, if possible, parents of minors upon whom they agreed to perform abortions. The Court denied the standing[15] of H. L., a 15-year-old minor dependent upon her parents, to challenge the applicability of the statute to mature and emancipated minors. Accordingly, the holding in *Matheson* was narrow. The Court upheld the Utah statute only as it applied to immature, unemancipated minors dependent upon their parents. The Court reserved judgment on whether state interests in promoting family integrity and protecting minors' welfare would justify requirements for notification of the parents of a mature minor seeking an abortion.

13. *See infra* notes 63 and 64.
14. 450 U.S. 398 (1981) (hereinafter cited as *Matheson*).
15. *Standing* refers to the right to litigate a given issue, usually dependent upon having a direct interest that might be affected by legal resolution of the issue.

In its next major abortion decisions, the Supreme Court both reaffirmed *Roe v. Wade* and upheld the *Bellotti* plurality's standard for a parental consent statute with a judicial bypass procedure. In *City of Akron v. Akron Center for Reproductive Health*,[16] the ordinance in question prohibited a physician from performing an abortion on a minor under age 15 unless the physician obtained written consent from the parents or a court order. The absolute parental veto established by this provision was in direct contradiction to *Bellotti*, because minors under 15 had no alternative means to obtain a determination of maturity. In sum, the Court found that Akron violated minors' right to privacy, as set forth in *Danforth* and *Bellotti*, by its blanket determination that *all* minors under age 15 are too immature to make the abortion decision or that an abortion without parental consent may never be in their best interests.

In *Planned Parenthood of Kansas City v. Ashcroft*,[17] a companion case to *Akron*, the Supreme Court considered the constitutionality of a Missouri statute that provided all minors with the opportunity to obtain an initial judicial determination of maturity. In upholding the constitutionality of the statute, the Court reiterated the standards outlined in *Bellotti*. The valid judicial bypass procedure provided a pregnant minor who elected not to seek parental consent with an alternative avenue (i.e., petition to the juvenile court) whereby she could demonstrate that she was sufficiently mature to make the abortion decision herself or, alternatively, that despite her immaturity, an abortion would be in her best interests.

An obvious theme in the minor abortion cases has been a differentiation between mature and immature minors. The emphasis probably has its roots in the *mature minor rule* that has been a feature of the law governing minors' consent to health care in some states (see Wadlington, 1973, 1983). This rule, which arose in judicial action but has been legislatively enacted in some jurisdictions, has its origins in the common-law doctrine of informed

16. 103 S.Ct. 2481.
17. 103 S.Ct. 2517 (1983) (hereinafter cited as *Ashcroft*).

consent. Before rendering treatment, a health professional is required to obtain consent from the patient for the proposed procedure. The consent, to be valid, must be voluntary, the product of adequate disclosure, and rendered by a competent individual. Because minors are generally presumed to be incompetent, they usually are precluded from legally authorizing their own treatment. However, "in a sense of judicial or legislative pragmatism" (Wadlington, 1973, p. 61), courts have tended to recognize consent to health care by competent adolescents in some situations. Nonetheless, courts and legislatures have rarely given clues as to the standard to be used for assessing competence and the reasons for the standard (cf. Weithorn, 1982).

Unfortunately, the Supreme Court has been no clearer in indicating the meaning of "maturity" in the context of abortion decisions. The *Matheson* dissenters indicated that they understood minors to be mature who are "capable of appreciating its [an abortion's] nature and consequences."[18] On the other hand, the *Matheson* majority seemed almost to equate maturity with emancipation (i.e., independence from parents in domicile and livelihood), but such an equation was never expressly stated. In the Missouri statute upheld in *Ashcroft*, courts considering minor's petitions for an abortion were directed to hear evidence of "the emotional development, maturity, intellect, and understanding of the minor."[19] The Supreme Court did not indicate, though, why the Missouri inquiry was sufficient to protect mature minors' privacy. All that is known with certainty at present is that "maturity" cannot be determined simply by establishing an age cutoff below which minors are presumed to be immature.[20] The elements of maturity have never been clearly identified by the Court.

To summarize, minors have a constitutional right to privacy in abortion decisions. However, this right is more limited than for adult women. Parental involvement in minors' abortion decisions is

18. 450 U.S. at 451 n.49.
19. *Ashcroft*, 103 S.Ct. at 2526.
20. *Akron*, 103 S.Ct. at 2498.

constitutionally sanctioned in two instances. First, a state may require parental consent for abortion if it concomitantly allows minors to seek judicial authorization for the procedure in lieu of parental consultation. Furthermore, third-party decision making must be conditioned on a determination of the minor's maturity or, if she is immature, her best interests. Second, a physician performing an abortion on an unemancipated, immature minor may be required to notify her parents before the procedure. Although both kinds of regulation of minors' decisions are predicated on a determination of maturity, the Supreme Court has yet to make clear what the term means in the context of abortion decisions.

SUBSTANTIVE ISSUES

LEGAL ASSUMPTIONS

Having examined the ways the Supreme Court has treated abortion by minors differently from abortion by adult women, we turn now to the Court's justifications for the greater regulation of minors' abortion decisions. The plurality in *Bellotti v. Baird* suggested three reasons that in some circumstances might permit states to infringe upon minors' privacy and liberty in ways that would be unconstitutional if applied to adults: "the peculiar vulnerability of children; their inability to make critical decisions in an informed, mature manner; and the importance of the parental role in child-rearing."[21] On its face, each of these invites psychological inquiry. Nonetheless, the Supreme Court generally has avoided empirical analysis and instead has relied on the "pages of experience" to test the applicability of these assumptions in cases about the constitutionality of age-based discrimination (see Melton, 1983a, 1984a, 1984b; Perry & Melton, 1984). Basing judgments primarily on intuition, the majority of the Court clearly believe that all three reasons are valid bases for regulating minors' access to abortions in ways that would be unconstitutional if applied to adult women.

21. 443 U.S. at 634.

Vulnerability

In recent years the Court frequently has postulated exceptional vulnerability of minors[22] to justify age-graded laws.[23] At the same time, it has underestimated the psychological harm inflicted upon minors by treating them as de facto nonpersons. For example, the Court recently resurrected the specious argument that serious infringement upon liberty—in that instance preventive detention—is in reality a rather trivial matter for minors because "juveniles, unlike adults, are always in some form of custody."[24] Thus the paradox is that the Court sometimes has approved of "arbitrary methods destructive of personal liberty"[25] of minors while viewing them as especially vulnerable to psychological harm. It takes a rather curious logic to justify intrusions upon privacy on the basis of a "peculiar vulnerability" while also asserting that minors are *less* vulnerable than adults to a sense of degradation from such intrusions.

The same kind of inconsistent thinking is clear in the adolescent abortion cases. To ensure that pregnant minors' decisions about abortion are mature or in their best interests, the Court has approved some state statutes that require parental consent or judicial review of a minor's plans to have an abortion.[26] Although the judicial inquiry is intended to protect immature minors from harm, one actual effect of the procedure may be to subject them to substantially more anxiety, embarrassment, and sense of violation than if the judicial review were not required. While emphasizing the trauma allegedly caused in minors because of the abortion

22. Throughout this chapter, *minors* will be used in lieu of other legal terms (e.g., *children, infants*) that imply greater incompetence of adolescents than is in fact the case. *Cf.* Melton (1984a).

23. *See e.g.,* Globe Newspaper Co. v. Superior Court, 102 S.Ct. 2613, 2626 (1982) (dissenting opinion); Parham v. J. R., 442 U.S. 584, 603 (1979); Ginsberg v. N.Y., 390 U.S. 629 (1968).

24. Schall v. Martin, 52 U.S.L.W. 4681, 4684 (U.S. June 4, 1984).

25. N.J. v. T.L.O., 53 U.S.L.W. 4083, 4096 (U.S. Jan. 15, 1985) (dissenting opinion of Stevens, J.). *See also* Doe v. Renfrow, 451 U.S. 1022, 1027–1028 (Brennan, J., dissenting from denial of certiorari).

26. *See, e.g., Ashcroft,* 103 S.Ct. 2517 (1983); *Matheson,* 450 U.S. 398 (1981).

decision, the Court ignored the potential psychological consequences of having to go before a judge to have a private decision
validated.

Regardless of the inconsistency, it is clear that the majority of
the Court believes that abortion by adolescents entails great psychological risk. Writing for the majority in *H. L. v. Matheson*,
Chief Justice Burger asserted that "the medical, emotional, and
psychological consequences of an abortion are serious and can be
lasting; this is particularly so when the patient is immature."[27] It is
noteworthy that one of the two articles cited to support the conclusion that the psychological effects of abortion are "markedly more
severe" than effects on adults[28] was in fact an account of rather
unsystematic psychoanalytic impressions of a sample of adolescents who carried their pregnancies to term (Babikian & Goldman,
1971). The other (Wallerstein, Kurtz, & Bar-Din, 1972) reported
impressions of a clinical sample; the generalizability and rigor of
the findings are problematic (cf. Adler, 1981).

The Court also claimed, rather incredibly, that the psychological risks associated with adolescent abortion are much greater than
those that accrue from a minor's decision to carry her pregnancy to
term: "If the pregnant girl elects to carry her child to term, the
medical decisions to be made entail few—perhaps none—of the
potentially grave emotional and psychological consequences of the
decision to abort."[29]

Incompetence

Besides perceiving minors as exceptionally vulnerable, the Court
has been skeptical about many adolescents' ability to make reasoned decisions about abortion.[30] Noting that "[t]here is no log-

27. 450 U.S. at 411.
28. *Id.* at 411, n.20.
29. *Id.* at 412–413.
30. *See, e.g., Akron*, 103 S.Ct. at 2491, n.10; *Bellotti II*, 443 U.S. at 640;
Danforth, 428 U.S. at 91 (Stewart, J., concurring); *id.* at 95 (White, J., dissenting).
See also Parham v. J. R., 442 U.S. 584, 603 (1979) (most adolescents are unable to
make sound judgments about treatment).

ical relationship between the capacity to become pregnant and the capacity for mature judgment concerning the wisdom of an abortion,"[31] the Court has even questioned the ability of minors to provide an adequate medical history.[32] This doubt about adolescents' competence to make critical decisions dovetails with the Court's disdain for abortion clinics and the perfunctory counseling it believes takes place there.[33] Some justices, notably Justice Powell, doubt the wisdom of minors in making an initial choice of physician or clinic.[34] Thus there is a concern that minors are often incapable of choosing physicians who will assess and remediate their incompetence to make a reasoned decision about whether to terminate a pregnancy. Even if the physician chosen is caring and careful, though, he or she may not provide suffcent attention to the "moral and religious concerns" raised by abortion; in fact, "the most significant consequences of the [abortion] decision are not medical in character."[35] At least implicitly, the Court does not believe many minors competent to consider these factors independently.

The Court's emphasis on competence to make reasoned decisions emanates in part from its emphasis on the privacy of *decisions* about reproductive matters.[36] In that sense the constitutional right to privacy is related more to autonomy in private matters than to freedom from bodily intrusion per se. Therefore a minor incapable of exercising such autonomy would have a diminished interest in privacy.[37]

31. *Matheson*, 450 U.S. at 408.

32. *Id.* at 411; *but see id.* at 443 (Marshall, J., dissenting) (dissent joined by Brennan and Blackmun, J J.).

33. *See, e.g., id.*, at 410 *quoting Bellotti II*, 443 U.S. at 641, *Danforth*, 428 U.S. at 91; *and Matheson*, 450 U.S. at 420 n.8 (Powell, J., concurring).

34. *Bellotti II*, 443 U.S. at 640–641.

35. *Akron*, 103 S.Ct. at 249 n.10; *Matheson*, 450 U.S. at 403, *quoting Bellotti II*, 443 U.S. at 640; *Matheson*, 450 U.S. at 423 (Stevens, J., concurring in the judgment), *quoting Danforth*, 428 U.S. at 103.

36. *See Akron*, 103 S.Ct. at 2491 n.10, *citing* Whalen v. Roe, 429 U.S. 589, 599–600 nn.24–26 (1977).

37. There are essentially two theories underlying the purported relationship between competence and constitutional rights (Melton, 1984a). According to one

Adolescent Abortion: A Psycholegal Analysis

Family Integrity

Assuming incompetence of minors to make reasoned judgments and special vulnerability to harm resulting from unwise decisions, parents are usually entrusted with making such judgments or at least advising the minor about the proper course of action.[38] Parents are presumed in most circumstances to act in their children's best interests.[39] Moreover, parents' interests in the discipline and values of their children are themselves private and constitutionally protected.[40] The state has interests in the socialization of minors and the preservation of the family as a core institution in the society. The family acts as a buffer between the state and the individual and as the primary institution for inculcating societal values. Therefore the promotion of family integrity is generally perceived to be in the state's interest. Insofar as family integrity is a fundamental right, there may be a corresponding loss of autonomy for minors, who are subject to the control of their parents.

In *Danforth*, however, the Court seemed to reject the assumption of identity of interest between pregnant minor and parents, at least when the minor seeks not to involve her parents in the abortion decision:

One suggested interest [in conditioning abortions by minors on parental consent] is the safeguarding of the family unit and of parental authority. . . . It is difficult, however, to conclude that providing a parent with absolute power to overrule a determination, made by the physician and his minor patient, to terminate the patient's pregnancy will serve to strengthen the family unit. Neither is it likely that such veto power will enhance parental authority or control where the minor and the nonconsenting parent are so fundamentally in conflict and the very existence of the pregnancy already has fractured the family structure.[41]

theory, competence in decision making is a requisite for full membership in the moral community and therefore the rights accorded to persons. On the other hand, the concern with competence may be based on an assumption that immature minors will be prone to make bad decisions and are therefore vulnerable to harm.

38. *See, e.g.,* Parham v. J. R., 442 U.S. 584, 603 (1979).
39. *Id.* at 602.
40. *See* Roe v. Wade, 410 U.S. 113, 152–153 (1973), and cites therein.
41. 438 U.S. at 75.

The *Danforth* plurality's assumption of an inherent fractionation of interests between pregnant minors and their parents has given way in more recent cases to increasing solicitude for family integrity. Indeed, the prevailing assumption by a majority of the Court is that "parental consultation often is desirable and in the best interest of the minor."[42] The majority recognizes the promotion of family integrity as a legitimate state interest, *in addition to*—and therefore presumably independent of—the protection of adolescents.[43]

An interesting middle position is held by Justice Stevens, who rejects the assumption of unity of interests between parent and child in commitment decisions but accepts it in abortion decisions.[44] In fact, apparently unlike the majority of the Court,[45] he would permit the application of parental notice requirements to mature minors.[46] Justice Stevens acknowledges "[t]he possibility that some parents will not react with compassion and understanding upon being informed of their daughter's predicament or that, even if they are receptive, they will incorrectly advise her."[47] Nonetheless, on balance, he believes that legislatures may reasonably assume that a requirement of parental notice or consultation will typically result in a better-reasoned decision in those instances where the "parent-child relationship is [n]either (a) so perfect that communication and accord will take place routinely [n]or (b) so imperfect that the absence of communication reflects the child's correct prediction that the parent will . . . [act] arbitrarily to further a selfish interest rather than the child's interest."[48] Justice Stevens believes that most cases when pregnant minors choose not to inform their parents fit into such a category, in which commu-

---

42. *Matheson*, 450 U.S. at 409, *quoting Bellotti II*, 443 U.S. at 640.
43. *See, e.g., Akron*, 103 S.Ct. at 2500 n.32; *Matheson*, 450 U.S. at 411.
44. *Matheson*, 450 U.S. at 423–424 n.1 (opinion concurring in the judgment).
45. *See Akron*, 103 S.Ct. at 2499 n.31.
46. *Matheson*, 450 U.S. at 424–425.
47. *Id.* at 424.
48. *Id.* at 423, *quoting Danforth*, 428 U.S. at 103–104 (Stevens, J., dissenting).

nication is less than ideal but parents are interested in the welfare of their children and able to assist them.[49]

Just as the Court's views of the parental role in adolescents' decisions about reproductive matters have evolved toward encouragement of parental participation, so too have the views of legislatures. Not only have several states enacted a parental notice statute governing adolescent abortion, but Congress has amended Title X of the Public Health Service Act to require family planning clinics receiving federal funds to "encourage family participation."[50] The Reagan administration's interpretation of this language to require parental notice[51]—the "squeal rule"—stimulated a storm of protest, including 60,000 comments from individuals, 1,200 letters from organizations, thousands of signatures. Two federal circuit courts ultimately enjoined enforcement of the rule as inconsistent with Congress's intent to increase minors' access to family planning services.[52]

Summary

Although the Court is far from single-minded in its approach to adolescent abortion cases,[53] it is clear that the majority finds ample basis for age-based regulation of abortion. The majority perceives pregnant minors as likely to make poorly reasoned decisions, ab-

49. *Matheson,* 450 U.S. at 423–424.

50. *See, e.g.,* 42 U.S.C. § 300(a) (1982); ARIZ. REV. STAT. ANN. § 36-2152 (Supp. 1984); IDAHO CODE § 18-609(6) (Cum. Supp. 1984); MD. HEALTH CODE ANN. § 50-103 (1982 and Cum. Supp. 1984); MINN. STAT. ANN. §§ 144.343(2) and 144.343(3) (West Cum. Supp. 1985); MONT. CODE ANN. § 50-20-107 (1981); UTAH CODE ANN. § 76-7-304 (Repl. Vol. 1978).

51. *Parental Notification Requirements Applicable to Projects for Family Planning Services,* 42 CFR Part 59, 48 Fed. Reg. 3600 (Jan. 26, 1983).

52. N.Y. v. Heckler, 719 F.2d 1191 (2d Cir. 1983); Planned Parenthood Federation of America, Inc. v. Schweiker, 712 F.2d 650 (D.C. Cir. 1983).

53. Both *Bellotti II,* 443 U.S. 622, and *Ashcroft,* 103 S.Ct. 2517, were decided by pluralities. In both cases Justice Powell delivered the judgment of the Court, upholding the middle position of validating parental consent requirements, provided that an alternative decision maker is available. The initial recognition of minors' right to privacy in *Danforth,* 428 U.S. 52, was a five-to-four decision.

sent involvement by parents or other third parties (participants in the decision other than the minor and her physician). Moreover, the Court assumes great risk of severe and permanent emotional scars when a decision to abort is made in adolescence. We turn now to an examination of the validity of the Court's assumptions.

PSYCHOLOGICAL EVIDENCE

Vulnerability

In terms of medical risks, the Chief Justice's sanguine view of pregnancy carried to term and his fear about the dangers of abortion in adolescence are clearly misplaced. Teenagers are no more likely than adult women to suffer complications as a result of abortion. Moreover, the mortality rate from pregnancy *continuation* is five times higher for teenagers than the mortality rate associated with adolescent abortion (Cates, 1981). This finding is consistent with research showing that women carrying unwanted pregnancies—often the case in adolescent pregnancies (Russo, this volume)—are at special risk for medical complications (Cates, 1982).

Research on psychological risks is less clear and less extensive. Research on the psychological effects of abortion has frequently been marked by substantial attrition in follow-up, inconsistency of definition, and other methodological flaws (Adler, 1976; David & Friedman, 1973; David, Rasmussen, & Holst, 1981). Although relatively recent studies have tended to be better designed and less obviously subject to investigator bias (Adler, 1979), there still are few studies that have isolated the effects of age on response to abortion (Adler & Dolcini, this volume).

Nonetheless, there is sufficient evidence to refute the Court's assumption that the effects of abortion on adolescents are "grave" and "markedly more severe" than the effects on adults (see generally Adler & Dolcini, this volume). Although it is undeniable that the decision whether to abort is stressful, it is also clear that the modal response to abortion itself is relief (Adler & Dolcini, this volume; Olson, 1980; Osofsky, Osofsky, & Rajan, 1973). Although there is some evidence for relatively more negative effects on adolescents (e.g., Bracken, Hachamovitch, & Grossman, 1974), the magnitude of age differences is small, and reactions are generally mild. Although the somewhat more negative responses of adolescents may be related to developmental issues, the predominant factors seem to be ones related to adolescents' social situation rather than developmental differences per se (e.g., tendency to delay seeking an abortion; coercion by mother or others to have an abortion; see Adler & Dolcini, this volume). Regardless, severe responses are very rare. In an analysis of health registry data in Denmark for 1975, David et al. (1981) found only five admissions to psychiatric hospitals of females aged 19 or under who had had abortions within the past three months, a rate of 11.4 psychiatric admissions per 10,000 abortions.

That abortion is frequently a relatively benign alternative for pregnant adolescents is unsurprising when one considers the social consequences of becoming a teenage parent, all of which carry their own psychological effects (see generally Marecek, this volume; Scott, 1984). Adolescent parenthood typically results in lower educational attainment than for peers of similar socioeconomic background and academic/vocational aspirations before the pregnancy (Card, 1977). Adolescent mothers also find their ultimate occupational attainment, income, and economic self-sufficiency (i.e., ability to stay off public assistance) to be lower than that achieved by peers who delayed childbearing (Card, 1977; Marecek, 1979). Not surprisingly, marriages resulting from adolescent pregnancies tend to be unstable, and females who begin childbearing at an early age ultimately have more children than peers who delay childbearing (see Marecek, this volume, for review).

Ultimately, unwanted children themselves may be the victims of restrictive abortion policies. Although findings are mixed and sparse, children born to adolescent mothers may be at increased risk for a variety of psychological problems, including poor intellectual and academic performance, low self-control, and passivity (Marecek, this volume). Most directly to the point, a longitudinal study of children born to women denied abortions in Czechoslovakia (David & Matejcek, 1981) has shown that in their teen years unwanted children experience a relatively high incidence of referrals for mental health services, relatively low educational attainment, and relatively high maternal emotional rejection (especially of boys). David and Matejcek concluded that "[w]hile there is evidence in many individual cases of an eventual compensation for the original rejection on the part of the mother or both parents, the finding that group differences between the matched children are still apparent after 16–18 years of family life, and that these differences have actually widened, suggests that 'unwantedness' during early pregnancy constitutes a not negligible risk factor for the subsequent life of the child" (p. 34).

Incompetence

Just as there is no evidence for marked negative psychological effects of abortion in adolescence, there is no reason to believe that adolescents will be less competent than adult women in decision making about abortion. There is now a substantial literature showing that adolescents do not differ from adults in their ability to understand and reason about treatment alternatives (see, for reviews, Grisso & Vierling, 1978; Melton, 1981; Melton, 1984a, pp. 463–466; Melton, Koocher, & Saks, 1983; Weithorn, 1982; see also Weithorn & Campbell, 1982).

However, as the Supreme Court has noted,[54] there are major factors to be considered in making a decision about abortion beyond the medical risks and benefits involved in terminating or carrying a pregnancy. The social and moral dimensions of the decision are sufficiently unusual and the importance of the problem sufficiently great that research is needed with a specific focus on age-related changes in competence to consent to abortion. At present there is only one such study. In a comparison of minors and adults at three pregnancy clinics in California, Lewis (1980) found few age-related differences in knowledge of the law or factors af-

54. *See supra* note 35.

fecting the decision whether to abort, deliver and relinquish the baby, or keep the baby. Minors did not differ from adults in "the number of people consulted or expected to be consulted; the tendency to consult the boyfriend, the parents, or members of the peer group; the expectation that conflicting advice will be received from different sources; or the expectation that advice will favor continuation of pregnancy vs. abortion" (Lewis, 1980, p. 448). The major differences identified were ones that might be expected to follow logically from differences in minors' and adults' social status and economic situation. Minors were more likely than adults to perceive their decision as externally determined (e.g., the product of parental wishes), and they were less likely to expect to consult a professional about the decision (cf. Lewis, 1981).

If "maturity" in the abortion context means something other than the ability to understand and reason about factors relevant to the decision, then determination of the typical level of maturity of pregnant adolescents will be more difficult and value-laden. As some commentators (e.g., Mnookin, 1985) have noted, conservatives may regard any minor who becomes pregnant as "immature," and liberals may perceive any unmarried pregnant teenager who seeks an abortion as demonstrating a "mature" response to the situation. Assuming, though, that maturity may refer to general psychological competence rather than specific competence, it is noteworthy that comparisons of personality functioning between adolescents who abort and those who carry to term generally show more adaptive, healthier functioning in the former group (Dixon, 1977; Falk, Gispert, & Baucom, 1981; Kane & Lachenbruch, 1973).

Family Integrity

The Supreme Court has assumed that the involvement of parents in minors' decisions about abortions will usually be helpful. There is in fact evidence that the probability of a positive emotional response to abortion increases when adolescents feel supported by their parents in their right to make a decision and in the decision itself (Bracken et al., 1974; see Adler & Dolcini, this volume). Pregnant adolescents who decide to carry to term often find that they overestimate the negativity of their parents' reactions to their pregnancy (Furstenberg, 1976).

Even without legal requirements, pregnant adolescents *do* often consult their parents, though commonly not until after discussions with male partners and girl friends. Among minors who carry to term, parents are commonly among the last confidants to be informed of the pregnancy (Allen, 1980). Similarly, in a sample of minors attending an abortion clinic in Minneapolis/Saint Paul, 37% told their mothers and 26% told their fathers, but 71% had talked with their best girl friends about the pregnancy (Clary, 1982). In a Michigan sample of pregnant teenagers, few (14%) sought advice from parents when they first suspected they were pregnant; most consulted their male partner or a girl friend (Rosen, 1980). Once pregnancy was confirmed, 57% involved their parents in the decision. The figures for adolescents who decided to abort and those who decided to carry the pregnancy to term were similar.

Those minors who do consult their parents before an abortion tend to be those for whom parental support might be expected to be most important and who are most at risk for negative psychological effects of the procedure (Clary, 1982; Torres, Forrest, & Eisman, 1980). Mothers also seem to have greater influence when their daughters are experiencing substantial conflict about the decision (Rosen, 1980).

In Clary's (1982) sample, the most common reason for not informing mothers about the pregnancy and impending abortion was concern for the parents' feelings (i.e., disappointment, embarrassment), but about 30% failed to tell their parents because they feared negative results (i.e., physical punishment, retaliation). Minors were especially unlikely to inform their parents if they believed that one or both held strongly negative attitudes toward abortion.

It is impossible to know whether the adolescents' perceptions of the likelihood of hostile reactions from their parents were accurate. The evidence that adolescents who decide to carry to term often overestimated the negativity of their parents' reaction (Furstenberg, 1976) may not reflect the reality for adolescents who decide to abort without informing their parents. In some sense, however, it makes no difference. The *perception* of probable hostile—or even just disappointed—reactions in their parents might be enough to increase pregnant minors' delay in seeking medical attention if parental notification were required. Delay in seeking abortion is already a major problem with minors (Bracken & Kasl, 1975; see Russo, this volume, for review); such delay substantially increases the medical and psychological risks associated with abortion (Bracken et al. 1974; Cates, 1981; Osofsky, Osofsky, Rajan, & Spitz, 1975).

Whatever the accuracy of teenagers' fears, the idyllic picture of American family life portrayed by the Supreme Court clearly does not match contemporary reality (Melton, 1984b). For example, in Clary's (1982) study, one-third of the minors seeking abortion came from single-parent families, and another 13% declined to inform their fathers because "we don't get along."

Even under substantially less stressful conditions than a daughter's announcement that she is or may be pregnant, sexuality is usually not a comfortable topic for parents and daughters. Among a stratified random sample of mothers of 10- to 18-year-olds in Cincinnati, only 31.5% reported giving their daughters reading material about sexuality, while 36.7% reported having explained intercourse and only half had discussed birth control (Rothenberg, 1980; see also Fox & Inazu, 1980; Furstenberg, 1971). Instead, adolescents report receiving most of their knowledge about sex from friends and teachers. As one of us has noted elsewhere, "[i]t would be surprising to find that this view of sex as a forbidden topic [in the home] should suddenly turn toward open and detailed discussion of the options available to a pregnant adolescent" (Melton, 1983b, p. 471).

The distance between parent and adolescent in matters of sexuality is not entirely unhealthy. Maintenance of privacy—including privacy of information about personal matters—is an important aspect of individuation, a principal developmental task of adolescence (Melton, 1983b; Wolfe, 1979). Although it is unfortunate when adolescents cut themselves from sources of counsel about private decisions, it is equally unfortunate when authorities overlook adolescents' need for privacy. In that regard, confidentiality is the major reason for choice of family planning clinics by adolescents, especially whites (Zabin & Clark, 1983).

Finally, the Court's view of the family may underemphasize the real power differentials within families. As a matter of law and of social, psychological, and economic reality, adolescents are rarely free to overcome the expressed will of their parents. Justice Stevens's contention that "a woman intellectually and emotionally capable of making important decisions without parental assistance also should be capable of ignoring any parental disapproval"[55] does not comport with common sense. The Court majority has recognized this point by requiring an alternative of judicial review *before* parental consent is sought.[56] Nonetheless, the Court's approval of parental notice requirements, at least for some minors, seems implicitly to suggest a belief that minors could be reasonably expected to seek approval for an abortion through judicial review or other procedure established by the state even when parents object to plans for an abortion.

Summary

Although the research is scant on some issues, the available evidence raises substantial doubt about the validity of the premises underlying the Supreme Court's approval of age-based regulation of abortion. Contrary to the Court's assumption of marked vulnerability of minors who obtain abortions, age differences in response to abortion are small, and in any event most adolescents who obtain abortions report relief. Severe emotional reactions are very rare. On the other hand, deleterious psychosocial effects on

55. *Matheson*, 450 U.S. at 425 n.2 (opinion concurring in the judgment).
56. *See Ashcroft*, 103 S.Ct. 2517; *Bellotti II*, 443 U.S. 622.

many minors who complete their pregnancies are well documented. By the same token, the research on consent to medical treatment and the single study currently available on consent to abortion give no reason to doubt adolescents' competence to make decisions about continuation of pregnancy. Additional research focused on the special aspects of the abortion decision is needed, however. Finally, although the Court's view of the helpfulness of parents of pregnant adolescents is undoubtedly true in many cases, this idyllic view ignores the many variations in family life. Many teenagers seeking abortions believe that informing their parents, some of whom are staunch foes of abortion, would result in retaliation and effectively block access to abortion. The literature on parent-adolescent communication about sexuality also gives reason to doubt the helpfulness of many parents in advising their children about decisions regarding pregnancy.

PROCEDURAL ISSUES

Assuming for argument that the Supreme Court is correct in positing significant state interests in the regulation of adolescent abortion, there still remain questions of whether procedures can be developed that will vindicate such interests. Can minimally intrusive procedures closely related to the state's purposes be designed to protect adolescents and promote family integrity?[57] Although research on the various procedural alternatives is still quite limited, there is some empirical basis for answering several of the procedural questions.

THE IMPLEMENTATION OF THE MATURE MINOR RULE

By relying on a mature minor standard, the Court has implicitly concluded that such a standard is workable. If professionals re-

57. When a fundamental right is infringed, the state regulation is subject to strict scrutiny. That is, the state must justify its intrusion by a compelling interest, and the infringement must be closely related to the purpose and the least intrusive means of fulfilling the purpose. San Antonio Indep. School Dist. v. Rodriguez, 411 U.S. 1, 33–34 (1973); Shelton v. Tucker, 364 U.S. 479, 488 (1960).

sponsible for counseling adolescents are unable to distinguish reliably and validly between mature and immature minors, the standard established by the Court is practically useless and indeed destined to result in purely arbitrary judgments. Even if it is possible to attain reliability in assessment, the standard might fail if the assessment required a very intrusive, extensive evaluation. Such an assessment would itself be burdensome and violate privacy. As a matter of public policy, it would also be an unwise allocation of counselors' time.

At present, any attempt to evaluate these hypotheses would be purely speculative. No research has examined the reliability, validity, or process of determining maturity in abortion decisions. Until the Court clarifies precisely what is meant by the standard, any such research is likely to be of questionable meaningfulness.

In the meantime, the ambiguity of the standard may itself have undesirable effects. The Court has made clear in dicta that a parental notice requirement may not be constitutionally applied to mature minors.[58] The Court has also held, though, that states may require notice to parents of immature, unemancipated minors seeking an abortion.[59] Thus, in a state with such a requirement, physicians may be subject to criminal penalties for failing to inform the parents of an immature minor. On the other hand, to inform the parents of a mature minor without her permission would violate her constitutional rights, which in turn may be a violation of professional ethics (American Psychological Association, 1981, Principle 3c). When there is no clarity about what maturity means, or even whether it is possible to assess maturity reliably and validly, health professionals are faced with an uncomfortable dilemma, to say the least. A result may be reluctance to deal with cases in which minors' competence is uncertain.

THE EFFECTS OF PARENTAL NOTICE REQUIREMENTS

Unless it actually results in parental consultation, a parental notice requirement is a meaningless hurdle delaying or obstructing mi-

58. See supra note 45.
59. Matheson, 450 U.S. 398.

nors' access to abortion. Moreover, except insofar as the purpose is to protect family integrity (i.e., parental control) per se, a parental notice statute would be constitutional only if it actually results in better-reasoned abortion decisions. Otherwise no significant state purpose would be served.

There are no outcome studies available on notice statutes of the sort upheld in *Matheson*.[60] Nonetheless, there are several reasons to doubt their efficacy. As we have already noted, it seems naive to assume that parental notice is likely to result in open and reasoned discussion of all the options available to a pregnant adolescent. Moreover, though most parents might be supportive, it is also obvious that some will be retaliatory or obstructionist, especially if they are strongly opposed to abortion. Even if such a reaction would not actually occur, many pregnant minors clearly *perceive* that it would. The tragic irony is that parental notice statutes may actually heighten the medical and psychological risks for minors by stimulating additional delay (cf. Cates, 1981; Zabin & Clark, 1983) and inhibiting reasoned analysis of the various alternatives.[61]

EFFECTS OF JUDICIAL ALTERNATIVES

In response to the plurality's suggestions in *Bellotti v. Baird*,[62] a number of states have enacted parental notice[63] or consent[64] statutes that provide the option of "bypassing" parents and seeking approval for an abortion from a judge. As already noted, these statutes require a two-level inquiry. First, if the judge finds the minor to be mature, the minor's privacy must be respected. Sec-

60. UTAH CODE ANN. § 76-7-304 (Repl. Vol. 1978).

61. As a practical matter, parents' compelling an abortion may be of greater frequency than their inhibiting it (Scott, this volume), although cases rarely reach the courts in such an instance. *But see In re* Smith, 16 Md. App. 209, 295 A.2d 238 (1972).

62. 43 U.S. 622.

63. *See, e.g.*, ARIZ. STAT. ANN. § 36-2152 (Supp. 1984); MINN. STAT. ANN. §§ 144.343(2) and 144.343(3) (Cum. Supp. 1985).

64. *See, e.g.*, LA. STAT. ANN. § 40:1228.25.5 (Cum. Supp. 1983); MASS. GEN. LAW. ANN. Ch. 112 § 12S (1983); N.D. CENT. CODE ANN. § 14-02.1-03.1 (Repl. Vol. 1981); R.I. GEN. LAWS § 23-4.7-6 (Cum. Supp. 1982).

ond, if the minor is immature, the judge must determine whether an abortion would be in her best interests.

As a matter of practice, proceedings have turned out to be pro forma rubber stamps of minors' decisions. Most minors are found to be mature, and, perhaps unsurprisingly, abortions are almost always found to be in the best interests of immature minors. In Massachusetts between April 1981, when the *Bellotti*-style statute took effect, and February 1983, about 1,300 minors sought abortions through the judicial bypass procedure (Mnookin, 1985). In about 90% of cases, minors were found to be mature. In the remaining cases, all but five petitioners' requests for abortions were approved, according to a best-interests standard. In three of those cases the trial court's decision was overturned on appeal. In one case the judge invited the minor to seek approval from another judge, who granted the petition. In the remaining case the minor decided to go to a neighboring state for the abortion. Similar findings have been reported in Minnesota, where only five petitions were denied from 1981 to 1983 (Donovan, 1983).

About three-fourths of minors obtaining abortions in Massachusetts obtain parental consent without going to court (Mnookin, 1985). It is estimated that before the enactment of the statute, one-third to one-half of pregnant minors consulted their parents before having an abortion. However, it is unclear that the statute has in fact resulted in an increase in parental consultation. There has been a marked drop in the number of abortions performed on minors in Massachusetts, apparently as a result of their choosing to go to neighboring states and avoid the judicial bypass procedure (Donovan, 1983; Mnookin, 1985). An analogous drop of 33% was observed in Minnesota during the first full year of its judicial bypass statute (Donovan, 1983). It is not known whether the statutes are increasing the number of unwanted children born to teenagers.

There is evidence that the statutes are increasing delay in obtaining abortions and therefore increasing risk to minors (Donovan, 1983). Generally it takes several days to schedule a hearing. In some instances minors may have to travel several days to obtain access to the courts, because many judges who are opposed to abortion have recused themselves. Thus there is a de facto waiting period, making minors miss more school and therefore causing greater difficulty in maintaining privacy.[65] Moreover, the process—real or perceived—of obtaining a lawyer and going before a judge may be sufficiently formidable to deter many minors from promptly seeking a pregnancy test and, subsequently, an abortion.

No research has systematically examined the psychological effects of the judicial procedures on the minors who go through them. Most of the pregnant minors who choose the alternative of going to court are older adolescents (ages 16 and 17) who are most likely to be competent to consent to an abortion (see generally Melton, Koocher, & Saks, 1983). It is plausible that the process of preparing for court helps also to prepare for the abortion itself (cf. Meichenbaum, 1977, on stress inoculation). However, it is not intuitively clear that rehearsal for court increases the thought and care applied to the decision making itself (Donovan, 1983). Also, although lawyers and clerks of courts have worked hard in some jurisdictions to minimize the trauma of going to court, there still is cause to wonder whether the judicial procedure does not *heighten*, instead of diminish, the psychological risks attached to abortion for minors. Some anxiety, embarrassment, and even sense of degradation about discussing personal matters with a lawyer and the judge would not be surprising. It is possible that these issues are least significant, although still present, in jurisdictions that conduct abortion hearings in juvenile or family court (Donovan, 1983).

Research is needed to evaluate the effects of *Bellotti*-style statutes more extensively. However, the evidence available suggests that they have harmed rather than helped minors considering abortion. Nothing has yet been uncovered to contradict the view of Justice Stevens and three other justices:

It is inherent in the right to make the abortion decision that the right may be exercised without public scrutiny and in defiance of the contrary opin-

65. State-imposed waiting periods have been found to place an unconstitutional burden on women's access to abortion. *Akron*, 103 S.Ct. at 2503; Ind. Planned Parenthood Affiliates Ass'n, Inc. v. Pearson, 716 F.2d 1127 (7th Cir. 1983); Zbaraz v. Hartigan, 584 F. Supp. 1452 (1984).

ion of the sovereign or other third parties. . . . As a practical matter, I would suppose that the need to commence judicial proceedings in order to obtain a legal abortion would impose a burden at least as great as, and probably greater than, that imposed on the minor child by the need to obtain the consent of the parent. Moreover, once this burden is met, the only standard provided for the judge's decision is the best interest of the minor. That standard provides little real guidance to the judge, and his decision must necessarily reflect personal and societal values and mores whose enforcement upon the minor—particularly when contrary to her own informed and reasonable decision—is fundamentally at odds with privacy interests underlying the constitutional protection accorded to her decision.[66]

EFFECTS OF OTHER PROCEDURAL ALTERNATIVES

Although no state has adopted such a procedure, the Supreme Court has left the door open for states to require a proceeding before an "independent decision maker" other than a judge as an alternative to parental consent to an abortion.[67] No research has examined the likely effects of such a procedure, perhaps unsurprisingly, given that it is not known what sort of nonjudicial decision maker would be found constitutionally acceptable by the Supreme Court. However, some might desire a counselor or a doctor to act as "neutral factfinder," a role the Court has condoned in other contexts.[68] Mnookin (1985), for example, has viewed Justice Powell's opinion in *Bellotti* as "a high water mark of judicial arrogance" (p. 263), demonstrating "an unwarranted confidence in the ability of judges to make sound decisions on behalf of individual pregnant minors, and to make sound policy for our society as a whole" (p. 262).

66. 443 U.S. at 655-56 (opinion concurring in the judgment); *Ashcroft*, 103 S.Ct. at 2531-32 (Blackmun, J., dissenting, joined by Brennan, Marshall, and Stevens, JJ.).

67. *Ashcroft*, 103 S.Ct. at 2526 n.20.

68. *See, e.g.*, Parham v. J. R., 442 U.S. 584, 606–607 (1979) (admitting physician may serve as "neutral fact finder" to decide whether parents may "voluntarily" admit their child to a psychiatric hospital). For a list of cases in which the *Parham* holding has been applied, see Perry & Melton (1984, p. 659 nn.132–134).

There is some merit in Mnookin's position. As already noted, it was rather ingenuous to assume that judicial proceedings would result in careful decision making and reduction of stress for pregnant minors. However, we would caution about the need for research and serious reflection before simply substituting mental health professionals, for example, for judges. The question whether minors should be permitted access to abortion is not a scientific one. That mental health professionals are expert in counseling does not imply that they also have special expertise in moral/legal decisions. Moreover, to place clinicians into a quasi-judicial position might not facilitate pregnant minors' involvement in counseling. Indeed, such a dual role might actually inhibit a counseling relationship. The problem of *Bellotti*-style statutes might be the mandatory injection of a third-party decision maker, not *who* the third party is. If the goal is universal counseling, then it would be more direct and effective to require *counseling*, not third-party decision-making. Even in that context, though, attention needs to be given to the effects of making counseling *mandatory*. In formulating policy, careful attention needs to be given to the possible effects—both intended and unintended—of the alternatives.

REQUIREMENTS FOR COUNSELING

Outcome research on counseling of minors about abortion decisions is limited. There is some evidence, though, that counseling lessens negative emotional effects and promotes a sense of relief (Marcus, 1979) by helping to clarify alternatives and thus reducing ambiguity of expectations and, therefore, anxiety (cf. Dibner, 1954). For those adolescents seeking abortion without parental consent, the need for, and utility of, counseling may be especially great. There may be fractionation of the family, making counseling useful regardless of whether an abortion is sought.[69] In such an instance the availability of an empathetic counselor also ensures

69. *See Akron*, 103 S.Ct. at 2502 n.38.

that there is *some* emotional and social support for the pregnant minor at a stressful time.

Although the research is limited, at least one study shows an age-related trend in preference for form of counseling. Younger pregnant women tended to prefer group rather than individual counseling (Bracken, Grossman, Hachamovitch, Sussman, & Schrieir, 1973). Insofar as the general literature on outcome of psychotherapy and counseling can be generalized to abortion counseling, it would be expected that the efficacy of particular forms of counseling would be related to the psychological and social characteristics of patients (cf. Bergin & Suinn, 1973; Gomes-Schwartz, Hadley, & Strupp, 1978)—"different strokes for different folks."

An implication of this literature is that though counseling should be available to those who wish it, the form and frequency of *mandatory* counseling should not be specified by law.[70] Not everyone needs or desires the same kind of information or support. Indeed, for a pregnant female already well informed, self-assured, and rational, *any* required counseling may unduly invade privacy. On the other hand, some pregnant females need much more intensive counseling, and the state may have a sufficiently compelling interest in the decision to require counseling in such a case. Even in that instance, though, mandating the form of the counseling would be contrary to the state's purposes. Similarly, although the state may have an interest in ensuring the counseling skills and relevant knowledge of abortion counselors, it would unduly narrow the field to limit the range of acceptable counselors to a particular discipline. As the Supreme Court has concluded, "The State's interest is in ensuring that the woman's consent is informed and unpressured; the critical factor is whether she obtains the necessary information and counseling from a qualified person, not the identity of the person from whom she obtains it."[71]

70. *See id.* at 2500–2501. Similar arguments were made in the *Akron* brief of amicus curiae Am. Psychological Ass'n.

71. *Akron,* 103 S.Ct. at 2502; *see also* brief in *Akron,* of amicus curiae Am. Psychological Ass'n.

WHAT SHOULD PSYCHOLOGISTS DO?

As the preceding review of the state of knowledge about adolescent abortion indicates, legal policy has often been grounded on assumptions that do not withstand empirical scrutiny or for which there is no empirical evidence. Whatever the wisdom of existing law, however, psychologists must of course assist their adolescent clients within that legal context. This context is often ambiguous and complex, and the underlying moral issues are themselves difficult. Counseling adolescents about abortion decisions (or conducting related research) thus requires extraordinary attention to ethical concerns (see Scott, this volume).

Respect for personal autonomy and privacy demands support for freedom of choice in decisions of great personal significance, like abortion. This general principle is consonant not only with psychologists' Ethical Principles (cf. APA, 1981, Preamble and Principles 3c and 6); it is also consistent with existing legal doctrine, which has been based on concern about the limits of adolescents' rational decision making. Within such an ethical and legal framework, psychologists counseling adolescents about an abortion decision have two principal tasks: to assist them in weighing the alternatives (e.g., abortion; completing the pregnancy and relinquishing the baby for adoption; completing the pregnancy and keeping the baby); and to provide emotional support so that they can make a sound personal decision under relatively unstressful conditions and so that they will not suffer untoward psychological sequelae of the decision itself.

In order to assist adolescents in decision making, psychologists must of course be willing to explore the alternatives (APA, 1981, Principle 6). Those whose moral scruples prevent such open discussion should so inform their clients and provide referrals to other counselors as needed. To preserve the range of options for minor clients, psychologists offering abortion counseling must know the alternatives. They should be able to explain the legal procedures in their jurisdictions for minors to obtain abortions with or without parental consent and to place a child for adoption.

In some jurisdictions, psychologists may be unable to guarantee confidentiality to minors who seek counseling about abortion. These constraints should be made clear to clients when they initiate counseling (APA, 1981, Principle 5). When legal strictures are unclear (e.g., whether counseling by school psychologists is confidential; whether state-imposed parental notice requirements may be applied to mature minors and, if not, how "maturity" is to be assessed), legal advice should be sought (e.g., an attorney general's opinion). Psychologists should advocate laws that will safeguard their clients' privacy (APA, 1981, Principle 3d).

In jurisdictions where judicial permission is required for an adolescent to receive an abortion without parental consent, psychologists may be asked to determine whether the client is "mature" and whether an abortion would be in her best interests. These are legal and moral determinations about which psychologists and other health professionals have no special expertise (cf. Bonnie & Slobogin, 1980; Melton, Petrila, Poythress, & Slobogin, in press, chap. 1; Morse, 1978). Thus, although psychologists may be able to provide information that will be helpful to the court in making its decision, they should resist offering ultimate-issue opinions (opinions about whether the legal standards for "maturity" and "best interests" have been met).

There are still sizable gaps in what is known about alternatives for policy on adolescent abortion. For example, there have been few evaluations of the effects of the various limitations that states have imposed on minors' access to abortion. The literature on the psychology of pregnant adolescents' decisions is also still quite limited. Psychologists can and should conduct the research needed to answer these questions, which are crucial both to policy formulation and to the development of counseling techniques. However, it must be acknowledged that there are special ethical and practical problems in conducting such research. Can a minor who is able to consent to an abortion independently also consent to research about abortion? Federal regulations[72] permit minors to

72. 45 C.F.R. § 46.402(a) (1984).

consent to research independently and privately in such circumstances, but state laws may provide no specific imprimatur for an exception to the usual rule that minors are per se incompetent to consent to research (see Keith-Spiegel, 1983). In view of both the private nature of the decision involved and the societal interest in increasing knowledge about adolescent abortion, states clearly should permit minors to consent independently to research about abortion if they are able to demonstrate an understanding of the risks and benefits of the research (cf. APA, 1981, Principle 9). However, keeping in mind the emotional loading of the topic and the usual legal presumption that adolescents are incompetent to consent, psychologists conducting research on adolescent abortion should pay special attention to ethical issues in their research (APA, 1981, Principle 9a). In addition to the usual review by institutional review boards, researchers might consider establishing an independent advisory group to safeguard the welfare of participants.

What Should Policymakers Do?

Although the policy chosen is likely to have significant psychological consequences, the questions of whether family privacy is superior to individual privacy and of when abortion is to be permitted are issues of morality and law, not empirical psychological fact. However, insofar as the legal calculus is based on psychological assumptions, policymakers should stimulate and attend to relevant psychological research. In that regard there is little evidence to support age-graded policies about abortion; research supports neither the contention that adolescents are especially unlikely to make reasoned decisions about abortion nor the assumption that adolescents are vulnerable to serious psychological harm as a result of abortion.

Consideration should be given to abolishing mature minor standards determining whether minors are permitted to obtain an abortion without parental notification or consent. It is hard to imagine a minor too immature to make the decision but mature enough to rear a child. In any case, no research has been conducted to determine whether "maturity" can be reliably and validly assessed. In the absence of clear legal standards, it is probable that such assessments are often erroneous. In view of the time consumed in performing such assessments and their questionable validity, it is unclear whether a mature minor standard can be effectively implemented even if it makes sense in the abstract.

Finally, government should encourage the development of counseling services for pregnant adolescents and their families. As the Supreme Court has recognized, these services should be provided by professionals with special training in counseling. Competent counseling is likely to enhance the quality of adolescents' decision making and to minimize emotional strain. Support for research is also essential if counselors are to respond optimally to pregnant adolescents' needs for information and emotional support. Ironically, the policy of the current administration to provide few, if any, grants for abortion-related research and counseling services is apt to hamper efforts to help pregnant adolescents make careful and relatively unstressful decisions.

The Supreme Court has recognized that "there are few situations in which denying a minor the right to make an important decision will have consequences so grave and indelible" as when a minor is faced with an unwanted pregnancy.[73] Unlike some decisions, a decision about termination of pregnancy obviously cannot be postponed until she reaches majority. If she chooses to carry the pregnancy to term, her decision will have substantial long-term effects upon her own life and those of others. Moreover, because the decision involves control over her own body and the most private aspects of her life, it is especially sensitive. Respect for persons requires respect for privacy, no less for adolescents than for adults (Melton, 1983b, 1983c). Indeed, given the ambiguous sociolegal status of adolescents, privacy may have even more profound meaning for adolescents (Melton, in press; Wolfe, 1979). Public policy—and the professional activities of psychologists—

73. *Matheson*, 450 U.S. at 427 (Marshall, J., dissenting, joined by Brennan and Blackmun, JJ.); *Bellotti II*, 443 U.S. at 646 (Powell, J., for the plurality).

should be based on a recognition of the significance of privacy and of the need to assist adolescents in exercising choice about the most private aspects of their lives.

REFERENCES

Adler, N. E. (1976). Sample attrition in studies of psycho-social sequelae of abortion: How great a problem? *Journal of Applied Social Psychology, 6,* 240–257.

Adler, N. E. (1979). Abortion: A social-psychological perspective. *Journal of Social Issues, 35,* 100–119.

Adler, N. E. (1981). Sex roles and unwanted pregnancy in adolescent and adult women. *Professional Psychology, 12,* 56–66.

Allen, J. E. (1980). *Managing teenage pregnancy: Access to abortion, contraception, and sex education.* New York: Praeger.

American Psychological Association. (1981). Ethical principles of psychologists. *American Psychologist, 36,* 633–638.

Babikian, H. M., & Goldman, A. G. (1971). A study in teen-age pregnancy. *American Journal of Psychiatry, 128,* 755–760.

Bergin, A. E., & Suinn, R. (1973). Individual psychotherapy and behavior therapy. *Annual Review of Psychology, 24,* 509–556.

Bonnie, R. J., & Slobogin, C. (1980). The role of mental health professionals in the criminal process: The case for informed speculation. *Virginia Law Review, 66,* 427–522.

Bracken, M., Grossman, G., Hachamovitch, M., Sussman, D., & Shrieir, D. (1973). Abortion counseling: An experimental study of three techniques. *American Journal of Obstetrics and Gynecology, 117,* 10–19.

Bracken, M., Hachamovitch, M., & Grossman, A. (1974). The decision to abort and psychological sequelae. *Journal of Nervous and Mental Disorders, 15,* 155–161.

Bracken, M., & Kasl, S. (1975). Delay in seeking induced abortion: A review and theoretical analysis. *American Journal of Obstetrics and Gynecology, 121,* 1008–1019.

Card, J. J. (1977). *Consequences of adolescent childbearing for the young parent's future personal and professional life.* Palo Alto, CA: American Institutes of Research.

Cates, W., Jr. (1981). Abortions for teenagers. In J. E. Hodgson (Ed.),

Abortion and sterilization: Medical and social aspects (pp. 139–154). London: Academic Press.

Cates, W., Jr. (1982). Legal abortion: The public health record. *Science, 215*, 1586–1590.

Clary, F. (1982). Minor women obtaining abortions: A study of parental notification in a metropolitan area. *American Journal of Public Health, 72*, 283–285.

David, H. P., & Friedman, H. L. (1973). Psychosocial research in abortion: A transnational perspective. In H. J. Osofsky & J. D. Osofsky (Eds.), *The abortion experience: Psychological and medical impact* (pp. 310–337). Hagerstown, MD: Harper and Row.

David, H. P., & Matejcek, Z. (1981). Children born to women denied abortion: An update. *Family Planning Perspectives, 13*, 32–34.

David, H. P., Rasmussen, N. Kr., & Holst, E. (1981). Postpartum and postabortion psychotic reactions. *Family Planning Perspectives, 13*, 88–93.

Dibner, A. S. (1954). Ambiguity and anxiety. *Journal of Abnormal and Social Psychology, 56*, 165–174.

Dixon, V. L. (1977). Teenage pregnancy: A personality comparison of prenatal and abortion groups. *Dissertation Abstracts International, 38*, 168B.

Donovan, P. (1983). Judging teenagers: How minors fare when they seek court-authorized abortions. *Family Planning Perspectives, 15*, 259–267.

Falk, R., Gispert, M., & Baucom, D. H. (1981). Personality factors related to black teenage pregnancy and abortion. *Psychology of Women Quarterly, 5*, 737–746.

Fox, G. L., & Inazu, J. K. (1980). Mother-daughter communication about sex. *Family Relations, 29*, 347–352.

Furstenberg, F. F., Jr. (1971). Birth control experience among pregnant adolescents: The process of unplanned parenthood. *Social Problems, 19*, 192–203.

Furstenberg, F. F., Jr. (1976). The social consequences of teenage parenthood. *Family Planning Perspectives, 8*, 148–164.

Gomes-Schwartz, B., Hadley, S. W., & Strupp, H. H. (1978). Individual psychotherapy and behavior therapy. *Annual Review of Psychology, 29*, 435–471.

Grisso, T., & Vierling, L. (1978). Minors' consent to treatment: A developmental perspective. *Professional Psychology, 9*, 412–427.

Kane, F., & Lachenbruch, P. (1973). Adolescent pregnancy: A study of aborters and non-aborters. *American Journal of Orthopsychiatry, 43,* 796–803.

Keith-Spiegel, P. (1983). Children and consent to participate in research. In G. B. Melton, G. P. Koocher, & M. J. Saks (Eds.), *Children's competence to consent* (pp. 179–211). New York: Plenum.

Lewis, C. (1980). A comparison of minors' and adults' pregnancy decisions. *American Journal of Orthopsychiatry, 50,* 446–453.

Lewis, C. (1981). How adolescents approach decisions: Changes over grades seven to twelve and policy implications. *Child Development, 52,* 538–544.

Marcus, R. J. (1979). Evaluating abortion counseling. *Dimensions in Health Service, 56,* 16–19.

Marecek, J. (1979). Economic, social, and psychological consequences of adolescent childbearing: An analysis of the Philadelphia Perinatal Project. Technical report submitted to NICHD.

Meichenbaum, D. (1977). *Cognitive-behavior modification: An integrative approach.* New York: Plenum.

Melton, G. B. (1981). Children's participation in treatment planning: Psychological and legal issues. *Professional Psychology, 12,* 647–654.

Melton, G. B. (1983a). Children's competence to consent: A problem in law and social science. In G. B. Melton, G. P. Koocher, & M. J. Saks (Eds.), *Children's competence to consent* (pp. 1–18). New York: Plenum.

Melton, G. B. (1983b). Minors and privacy: Are legal and psychological concepts compatible? *Nebraska Law Review, 62,* 455–493.

Melton, G. B. (1983c). Toward "personhood" for adolescents: Autonomy and privacy as values in public policy. *American Psychologist, 38,* 99–103.

Melton, G. B. (1984a). Developmental psychology and the law: The state of the art. *Journal of Family Law, 22,* 445–482.

Melton, G. B. (1984b). Family and mental hospital as myths: Civil commitment of minors. In N. D. Reppucci, L. A. Weithorn, E. P. Mulvey, & J. Monahan, *Children, mental health, and the law* (pp. 151–167). Beverly Hills, CA: Sage.

Melton, G. B. (in press). Are adolescents people? Problems of liberty, entitlement, and responsibility. In J. Worell & F. Danner (Eds.), *Adolescent development: Issues for education.* New York: Academic Press.

Melton, G. B., Koocher, G. P., & Saks, M. J. (Eds.). (1983). Children's competence to consent. New York: Plenum.

Melton, G. B., Petrila, J., Poythress, N. G., Jr., & Slobogin, C. (in press).

Psychological evaluations for the courts: A handbook for mental health professionals and lawyers. New York: Guilford.

Mnookin, R. H. (1985). *Bellotti v. Baird:* A hard case. In R. H. Mnookin (Ed.), *In the interest of children: Advocacy, law reform, and public policy* (pp. 149–264). New York: W. H. Freeman.

Morse, S. J. (1978). Crazy behavior, morals, and science: An analysis of mental health law. *Southern California Law Review, 51,* 527–654.

Olson, L. (1980). Social and psychological correlates of pregnancy resolution among adolescent women: A review. *American Journal of Orthopsychiatry, 42,* 48–60.

Osofsky, J. D., Osofsky, H. J., & Rajan, R. (1973). Psychological effects of abortion: With emphasis upon immediate reactions and followup. In H. J. Osofsky & J. D. Osofsky, *The abortion experience: Psychological and medical impact* (pp. 188–205). Hagerstown, MD: Harper and Row.

Osofsky, J. D., Osofsky, H. J., Rajan, R., & Spitz, D. (1975). Psychosocial aspects of abortion in the United States. *Mount Sinai Journal of Medicine, 42,* 456–467.

Perry, G. S., & Melton, G. B. (1984). Precedential value of judicial notice of social facts: *Parham* as an example. *Journal of Family Law, 22,* 633–676.

Rosen, R. H. (1980). Adolescent pregnancy decision-making: Are parents important? *Adolescence, 15,* 43–54.

Rothenberg, P. B. (1980). Communication about sex and birth control between mothers and their adolescent children. *Population and Environment, 3,* 35–50.

Scott, E. S. (1984). Adolescents' reproductive rights: Abortion, contraception, and sterilization. In N. D. Reppucci, L. A. Weithorn, E. P. Mulvey, & J. Monahan (Eds.), *Children, mental health, and the law* (pp. 125–150). Beverly Hills, CA: Sage.

Torres, A., Forrest, J. D., & Eisman, S. (1980). Telling parents: Clinic policies and adolescents' use of family planning and abortion services. *Family Planning Perspectives, 12,* 284–292.

Wadlington, W. J. (1973). Minors and health care: The age of consent. *Osgoode Hall Law Journal, 11,* 115–125.

Wadlington, W. J. (1983). Consent to medical care for minors: The legal framework. In G. B. Melton, G. P. Koocher, & M. J. Saks (Eds.), *Children's competence to consent* (pp. 57–74). New York: Plenum.

Wallerstein, J., Kurtz, P., & Bar-Din, M. (1972). Psychosocial sequelae of therapeutic abortion in young unmarried women. *Archives of General Psychiatry, 27,* 828–832.

Weithorn, L. A. (1982). Developmental factors and competence to make informed treatment decisions. In G. B. Melton (Ed.), *Legal reforms affecting child and youth services* (pp. 85–100). New York: Haworth.

Weithorn, L. A., & Campbell, S. B. (1982). The competency of children and adolescents to make informed treatment decisions. *Child Development, 53,* 1589–1599.

Wolfe, M. (1979). Childhood and privacy. In I. Altman & J. F. Wohlwill (Eds.), *Human behavior and environment: Advances in theory and research* (Vol. 3, pp. 175–222). New York: Plenum.

Zabin, L. S., & Clark, S. D., Jr. (1983). Institutional factors affecting teenagers' choice and reasons for delay in attending a family planning clinic. *Family Planning Perspectives, 15,* 25–29.

NANCY FELIPE RUSSO

Adolescent Abortion: The Epidemiological Context

During the 1970s, teenage pregnancy rates increased. At the same time, however, numbers and rates of teenage births declined. This seemingly paradoxical effect reflects the significant role that abortion plays in the control of adolescent childbearing. Of the 1.1 million teenage pregnancies in 1981, more than 39% were terminated by abortion. About 47% ended in live births, one-half of them to unmarried women; 14% resulted in miscarriages (Alan Guttmacher Institute [AGI], 1983).

The large number and proportion of teenage pregnancies terminated by abortion increases the importance of understanding the abortion experience in adolescence. As an initial step toward that understanding—which ultimately must encompass biological, psychological, social, and cultural analyses—this chapter provides an overview of the available demographic and epidemiological findings on teenage abortion since 1973, the year of the Supreme Court decision legalizing that procedure.

Interpreting demographic and epidemiological data on teenage abortion over time is a complex task. The number of teenagers varied widely during the 1970s as the cohorts of baby boom babies passed through their adolescent years. More adolescents became sexually active at younger ages, increasing their risk of pregnancy faster than access and use of contraceptives could decrease that risk (AGI, 1981).

Difficulty in interpretation is compounded by the lack of data reported by single year of age within the age range 15–19. Issues related to reproductive outcome, informed consent, and parental notification are different for younger (under 15 years), middle (15–17 years), and older (18–19 years) teenagers. As Baldwin (1982) has pointed out, aggregating teenagers aged 15–19 includes age groups with different prospects for good medical outcomes, married with unmarried, and high-school graduates with students who have yet to complete their secondary education. Adolescents under age 18—and those aged 18–19 who have already had a child—are of particular concern, since they are at risk for medical and social problems associated with childbearing (McCormick, Shapiro, & Starfield, 1984).

SOURCES AND LIMITATIONS OF ABORTION DATA

Difficulties in interpreting abortion data are compounded by methodological problems. Abortion data are difficult to collect, and national statistics can only be considered estimates. The figures below are primarily based on data provided by the Alan Guttmacher Institute (AGI), the most comprehensive source of national abortion statistics. AGI data are based on national surveys of health institutions and private physicians providing abortion services. Since 1977 the National Center for Health Statistics has also reported abortion data, but only about one in four states is included in the reporting area. In addition, the Centers for Disease Control (CDC) reports abortion surveillance data obtained from central state agencies and from hospitals or facilities in which abortions are performed. Its most recent publication reports 1980 abortion surveillance data by a variety of demographic characteristics (CDC, 1983). That year an estimated 29% of the 1,297,606 abortions reported to the CDC were performed on teenagers, a proportion similar to the 28.5% reported by the AGI.

The number of abortions identified by the CDC is less than the number actually performed, because it is based on data reported by health agencies and does not include direct surveys of physician providers. For 1980, CDC's total was 20% lower than the total reported by AGI.

More than 8 out of 10 of the reported abortions to teenagers aged 15–19 take place in freestanding clinics (Henshaw & O'Reilly, 1983). As Tietze (1983) pointed out, underreporting is probably lowest in areas where abortion must be performed in licensed facilities and where a formal authorization procedure is required by law. Underreporting is probably greater for abortions performed by private practitioners in their offices or surgeries.

Because the number of states reporting demographic characteristics to the CDC varies from year to year, comparisons over time must be made with caution. Legal or financial considerations may bias the reporting of personal characteristics such as age, weeks of gestation, and residence. Marital status and number of prior induced abortions may also be misstated because of embarrassment. These methodological limitations should be kept in mind when drawing conclusions from abortion statistics from any source.

TEENAGE ABORTION: A PROFILE

NUMBERS AND DISTRIBUTION

A substantial number and proportion of abortions are obtained by teenagers. According to AGI, in 1981 more than 1 in 4 (28.5%) of the estimated 1,577,340 abortions performed were to teenagers; 6 out of 10 abortions to 15–19-year-olds were to teenagers 18–19 years of age. Table 1 lists the number and distribution of legal abortions, abortion rates per 1,000 women, and percentage of pregnancies terminated by abortion, by age group from 1973 to 1981.

The number of teenage abortions has risen since the Supreme Court decision in 1973, but not as rapidly as the number of abortions to other women of childbearing age. From 1973 to 1981, the number of abortions to women aged 20–44 went from 744,610 to 1,577,340, a rise of 112%. In contrast, the number of abortions to teenagers increased from 244,070 to 448,570, a rise of 84%.

The increase in number of abortions has been greater for older teenagers. Between the ages of 15 and 19, the number of abortions went from 232,440 in 1973 to 433,330 in 1981, an increase of 86%. Below age 15, the increase was 31%, from 11,630 to 15,240. Figure I shows the change in the number of teenage abortions by year since 1973 for the three age groups: below 15, 15–17, and 18–19. The numbers for teenagers below 15 have stayed about the same, while those for the other two groups have increased and then dropped slightly.

The proportion of total abortions that are obtained by teenagers has declined slightly. From 1973 to 1981, for teens aged 15–19, the proportion fell from 31.2% to 27.5%. For teenagers under age 15, the decline was from 1.6% to 1.0%. This largely reflects the change in the age distribution of women, since teenagers continue to have the highest abortion/live birth ratio (except for women over 40).

FIGURE I

Number of abortions among teenagers, in thousands, by age group: United States, 1973–1981. Data from Alan Guttmacher Institute.

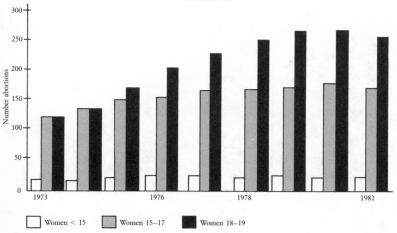

TABLE I

Number of Legal Abortions, Abortion Rate per 1,000 Women, and Percentage of Pregnancies Terminated by Abortion, by Age, United States, 1973–1981

	1973	1974	1975	1976	1977	1978	1979	1980	1981
	Number of Abortions								
Total	744,610	898,570	1,034,170	1,179,300	1,316,700	1,409,600	1,497,670	1,553,890	1,577,340
Below 15	11,630	13,420	15,260	15,820	15,650	15,110	16,220	15,340	15,240
15–19	232,440	278,280	324,930	362,680	396,630	418,790	444,600	444,780	433,330
15–17	n.a.	n.a.	n.a.	(152,700)	(165,610)	(169,270)	(178,570)	(183,350)	(175,932)
18–19	n.a.	n.a.	n.a.	(209,980)	(231,020)	(249,520)	(266,030)	(261,430)	(257,398)
20–24	240,610	286,600	331,640	392,280	449,660	489,410	525,710	549,410	554,940
25–29	129,600	162,690	188,900	220,500	246,680	265,990	284,200	303,820	316,260
30–34	72,550	89,810	100,170	110,050	124,380	134,280	141,970	153,060	167,240
35–39	40,960	48,770	52,740	56,720	61,700	65,350	65,070	66,580	69,510
40 or over	16,820	19,000	20,530	21,250	22,000	20,670	19,900	20,900	20,820

continued

TABLE I, CONTINUED

	1973	1974	1975	1976	1977	1978	1979	1980	1981
	Abortion Rate[a]								
Total	16.3	19.3	21.7	24.2	26.4	27.7	28.8	29.3	29.3
Below 15	5.6	6.4	7.2	7.6	7.6	7.5	8.3	8.4	8.6
15–19	22.8	26.9	31.0	34.3	37.5	39.7	42.4	42.9	43.3
15–17	(18.7)	(22.3)	(24.1)	(24.2)	(26.2)	(26.9)	(28.8)	(30.2)	(30.1)
18–19	(28.9)	(34.3)	(41.9)	(49.3)	(54.1)	(58.4)	(61.9)	(60.9)	(61.8)
20–24	26.2	30.4	34.3	39.6	44.3	47.2	49.9	51.4	51.1
25–29	16.4	19.6	21.8	24.1	26.9	28.4	29.6	30.8	31.4
30–34	10.9	13.0	14.0	15.0	15.7	16.4	16.5	17.0	17.7
35–39	7.1	8.4	8.9	9.3	9.8	9.8	9.4	9.3	9.5
40 or over	2.9	3.3	3.6	3.7	3.9	3.6	3.4	3.5	3.4

continued

TABLE I, CONTINUED

Percentage of Pregnancies Terminated by Abortion[b]

	1973	1974	1975	1976	1977	1978	1979	1980	1981
Total	19.3	22.0	24.9	26.5	28.6	29.2	29.6	30.0	30.0
Below 15					41.1	40.9	43.0	41.7	43.3
15–19	25.6c	29.0c	33.4c	35.8c	38.3	39.5	40.6	40.5	40.6
15–17	n.a.	n.a.	n.a.	n.a.	(38.7)	(39.7)	(41.3)	(41.7)	(41.7)
18–19	n.a.	n.a.	n.a.	n.a.	(37.9)	(39.3)	(40.1)	(39.6)	(39.9)
20–24	17.6	20.0	22.8	25.0	27.6	28.7	29.4	29.9	30.2
25–29	13.2	15.4	17.2	18.6	20.2	20.8	21.1	21.9	22.1
30–34	18.7	21.7	23.5	23.1	23.7	23.5	23.0	23.8	24.2
35–39	26.3	32.8	35.4	36.6	38.5	38.6	37.3	37.4	37.5
40 or over	39.7	44.4	48.6	50.2	52.5	51.6	50.4	51.7	51.1

continued

ᵃDenominator for total abortion rate is women aged 15–44.

Numerator is abortions obtained by girls younger than 15; denominator is number of 14-year-old females.

Numerator is abortions obtained by women 40 and over; denominator is women aged 40–44.

ᵇDenominator is live births six months later (to match time of conception with abortions) and abortions.

Pregnancies exclude miscarriages and stillbirths. Births and abortions are ad-justed to age of women at time of conception.

ᶜFrom 1973 to 1976, figures include women with age under 15 through age 19. For 1977 to 1981, figures are broken down.

SOURCES: Number of abortions, by age, 1974–1978: *Abortion 1977–1979: Need and Services in the United States, Each State and Metropolitan Area*, by S. K. Henshaw, J. D. Forrest, E. Sullivan, and C. Tietze, 1981 (New York: Alan Guttmacher Institute), Table 11–3. Number of abortions, 1979–1980: total from AGI survey and characteristics from CDC, Abortion Surveillance, Annual Summary, 1979–1980, Atlanta, 1983, with adjustments for changes in states reporting data to the CDC each year. Population data: from U.S. Bureau of the Census, "Preliminary Estimates of the Population of the United States, by Age, Sex, and Race: 1970 to 1981," 1982, *Current Population Reports*, Series P-25, No. 917, Table 2. Percentage of pregnancies terminated by abortion: *Induced Abortion: A World Review, 1983*, 1983 (New York: Population Council). Unpublished data for 1981 provided by Asta Kenney and Stanley Henshaw, Alan Guttmacher Institute.

Note. n.a. = not available.

ABORTION RATES

Numbers of abortions are useful in assessing demand for services, the need for trained personnel and facilities, and so forth. Abortion rates—number of abortions per 1,000 women—help us understand the extent of the demand for abortion among the female population.

Teenagers between 18 and 19 years of age have the highest demand for abortion services for women of any age, at 61.8 per 1,000 in 1981. For teenagers aged 15–17 years, the rate was 30.1; for teenagers below age 15, it was 8.6. (See Table 1.)

The rise in teenage abortion rates has been greater than that for women of childbearing age overall. Between 1973 and 1981, abortion rates for teenagers between 15 and 19 years went from 22.8 to 43.3, an increase of 90%. For teenagers below 15, the increase was 54%, from 5.6 to 8.6. In comparison, the increase for all females of childbearing age was 80%, from 16.3 to 29.3. Figure 2 shows the change in abortion rates from 1973 to 1981, by age group where data are available.

PERCENTAGE OF PREGNANCIES TERMINATED BY ABORTION AND ABORTION RATIOS

Among sexually active women who wish to avoid pregnancy but do not practice effective contraception, the percentage of pregnancies terminated by abortion is high because many unwanted pregnancies are aborted. The difference between the two statistics reflects differences in both sexual activity and use of contraception. Women who are effective contraceptors have fewer unwanted pregnancies and, consequently, have both a lower abortion rate and a lower proportion of terminated pregnancies.

Computing the percentage of pregnancies terminated by abortion involves considerable error in estimating the denominator, because an estimate of the proportion of pregnancies lost through miscarriage must be included. The failure to include illegal abortions can be another source of error in estimating the denominator.

FIGURE 2

Abortion rates among teenagers, by age group: United States, 1973–1981. Data from Alan Guttmacher Institute.

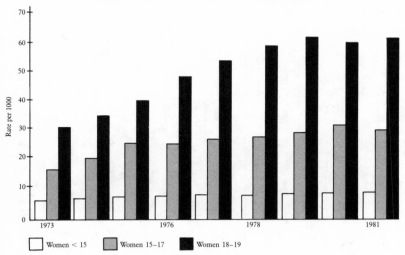

The ratio of abortion to live births has the advantage that the denominator can be estimated within narrow limits (Tietze, 1983).

The role of abortion in controlling unwanted pregnancy for teenagers has increased, and abortion ratios for live births have risen since 1973 for all three adolescent age groups. Figure 3 shows the change in abortion ratios from 1973 to 1981. For 1973, the percentage of pregnancies terminated by abortion for teenagers overall was 25.6. In 1981, the percentage for teenagers aged 15–19 was 40.6.

The difference between abortion rate and ratio of abortions to live births varies markedly by age group. When a birthrate is low, as for younger teenagers, the corresponding abortion ratio is higher. Note: in computing the ratio of abortions to live births, in order to approximate distribution by age at conception, the denominator used was abortions plus live births six months later.

The younger the teenager, the greater the role of abortion in

FIGURE 3

Number of abortions among teenagers per 1,000 live births by age group, 1973–1981. Data from Alan Guttmacher Institute.

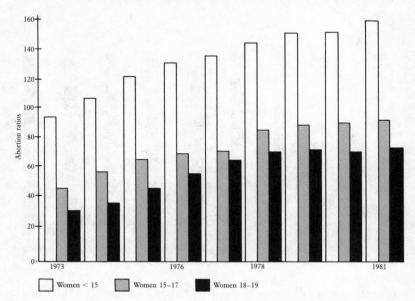

 fertility control. In 1981, for ages 18–19, 39.9% of pregnancies were terminated by abortion; for teenagers between 15 and 17, the figure was 41.7%. For teenagers below age 15, the figure was 43.3%. This is the highest proportion for any age group except women 40 and over, who terminated 51.1% of pregnancies by abortion.

CHARACTERISTICS OF TEENAGERS OBTAINING ABORTIONS

The following discussion focuses on the characteristics of individuals receiving abortions in 1980 and 1981, the most recent years for which detailed data are available (CDC, 1983; Henshaw &

O'Reilly, 1983). Unless otherwise noted, the data come from the 84% of the 1980 CDC data for which age at abortion was reported.

Race/Ethnicity

Nonwhites. Of the 33 states reporting to the CDC, nonwhites (92% of whom are black) obtained 48.1% of the 7,701 abortions to adolescents under 15 years of age. In contrast, they obtained 25.3% of the 222,264 abortions to adolescents between 15 and 19 years old.

Abortion rates among black teenagers have been consistently higher than those among white teenagers, and the differentials have widened. From 1972 to 1978, the adolescent abortion rate per 1,000 blacks aged 12–19 went from 17.4 to 51.2; for whites the rate went from 11.7 to 24.3 (Ezzard, Cates, Kramer, & Tietze, 1982; see Figure 4).

The younger the adolescents, the greater is the racial difference in abortion rate. The largest difference is among black teenagers below age 15, where the abortion rate for 1978 was five times higher than among whites (24.4 vs. 5.0). When abortion rates are calculated using only sexually active teenagers as the base, blacks aged 18–19 have higher abortion rates than blacks aged 15–17. The reverse pattern is true for whites (Henshaw & O'Reilly, 1983).

The accelerated use of legal abortion by black teenagers lessened both their rates of unmarried childbearing and their rates of illegal abortion. Before 1972, the birthrates of unmarried women had been rising in states where abortion was illegal. Since 1973, however, birthrates for unmarried black teenagers have leveled off. Further, between 1972 and 1974, when abortion rates for black teenagers increased sharply, deaths from illegal abortion declined more rapidly among blacks than among whites (Ezzard et al., 1982).

To understand intergroup comparisons of abortion rates and ratios, it is important to take into account both risk of pregnancy and likelihood of choosing to bear a child once pregnant. There are substantial differences in fertility-related behavior between blacks and whites. Compared with white adolescents, higher proportions

FIGURE 4

Estimates of abortion rates per 1,000 women aged 12–19 (age at conception), by race: United States, 1971–1978. Data from "Race-Specific Patterns of Abortion Use by American Teenagers," by N. V. Ezzard, W. Cates, Jr., D. G. Kramer, and C. Tietze, 1982, *American Journal of Public Health, 72,* 809.

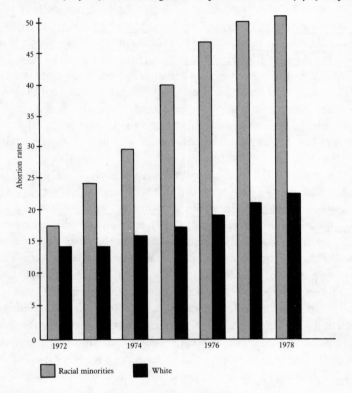

of black teenagers become sexually active at younger ages, lack knowledge of birth control, use less effective methods of contraception, and delay initiation of contraception after intercourse (Ezzard et al., 1982).

These conditions lead to unintended pregnancy, and abortion

rates are higher for black adolescents because they have more unintended pregnancies. However, racial differences in the percentage of pregnancies terminated by abortion have decreased. There has been a consistent increase in the ratio of abortions to live births among both black and white adolescents. In 1972, ratios for blacks were lower than those for whites. By 1978, the ratios became similar for the two racial groups, so that now, given a pregnancy occurs, black teenagers choose abortion only slightly more often than their white counterparts (Henshaw & O'Reilly, 1983).

Despite higher abortion rates, fertility rates for blacks are 37% higher than such rates for whites (Henshaw & O'Reilly, 1983). Black teenagers account for one-fourth of all black childbearing. The fertility rate of blacks is seven times that of whites in the 10- to 14-year age group. Among 15- to 19-year-olds, black teenagers are more likely than whites to carry a pregnancy to term and less likely to place for adoption a child born out of wedlock. On the average, black teenagers have twice as many children as their white peers by the time they reach 20 years of age (Westoff, Calot, & Foster, 1983).

In fact, in a comparison of teenage fertility rates of 32 developed countries, which also reported separate rates for United States blacks and Israeli Arabs, the teenage fertility rate for United States blacks was substantially higher than teenage fertility rates in any of the countries studied. At 515 per 1,000 in 1979/1980, the fertility rate for black teenagers in the United States exceeded even the rate of Arab teenagers living in Israel, who marry very young (Westoff et al., 1983).

Hispanics. The Hispanic population is the fastest-growing minority group in the United States, with a birthrate 75% higher than that of the rest of the population (Center for Population Options, 1984). Although national statistics are not available for Hispanics, in 1980, 68% of Hispanic adolescents in New York City terminated their pregnancies by abortion, compared with 57% of black and 53% of white adolescents in that city (New York State Council on Children and Families, 1984).

Marital Status

A majority of teenage abortions are obtained by unmarried women (i.e., never married, separated, divorced, or widowed), and abortion rates are higher for unmarried than for married teenagers overall (43 vs. 31 per 1,000). This pattern reflects the large differential for 18- to 19-year-olds, however, and does not hold for teenagers aged 15–17. In 1979, for ages 18–19, the abortion rate for 1,000 unmarried women was 67, compared with a rate of 30 for married women. For ages 15–17 the pattern was reversed. The rate for unmarried women was 29 compared with a rate of 36 for married women (Henshaw & O'Reilly, 1983; see Figure 5).

This reversal reflects an increase in sexual activity that occurs for 18- to 19-year-olds. As Henshaw and O'Reilly (1983) point out,

FIGURE 5

Abortion rates among teenagers, by age group and marital status, 1981. Data from "Characterization of Abortion Patients in the United States, 1979 and 1980," by S. K. Henshaw and K. O'Reilly, 1983, *Family Planning Perspectives, 15*, 5–15.

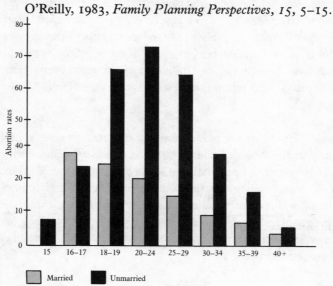

if the abortion rate were based only on sexually active unmarried women between the ages of 15 and 17, it would have been at least 79 per 1,000—greatly exceeding the rate of 36 for their married counterparts. For both married and sexually active unmarried women, the abortion rate is highest among teenagers, falling sharply with age.

Residence

There has been no systematic evaluation of how geographic availability of abortion services to teenagers differs from availability of such services to older women. We do know that there are wide variations in the geographical availability of abortion services. They are most available in states on the East and West coasts, and abortion rates are highest in those states (Henshaw, Forrest, & Blaine, 1984). The proportion of abortions performed on teenagers also varies by state and does not correspond with the overall abortion rate. For example, in 1980 Arkansas had the fifth-lowest abortion rate (a tie with Utah at 12.3 per 1,000 women aged 15–44). Yet Arkansas had the highest percentage of abortions performed on teenagers, at 35.6%.

The proportion of abortions performed on teenagers varies from that high of 35.6% in Arkansas to a low of 23.5% in the District of Columbia. Arkansas, Kansas, Minnesota, Nebraska, North Dakota, and South Dakota all had more than one in three abortions performed on females 19 years of age or younger. California had the largest number of abortions to teenagers (59,788), followed by New York (36,985).

Of the 41 states for which data are available, 12—California, Georgia, Illinois, Maryland, Massachusetts, Michigan, New York, North Carolina, Ohio, Pennsylvania, Virginia, and Washington—account for 70% of abortions to teenagers (219,682). Unfortunately, figures for Texas were not included in the CDC data, since AGI figures show Texas to have the third-highest number of overall reported abortions in 1980 (102,000) after California (262,710) and New York (187,460) (Henshaw et al., 1984).

Lack of accessible abortion services contributes to interstate variations in fertility. In 1982, 78% of all United States counties had no identified provider, and 28% of women of childbearing age resided in those counties. Although 26% of women aged 15–44 lived outside metropolitan areas, only 87% of the counties in such areas had abortion service providers. Even in urban areas, where abortion services are concentrated, 57% of metropolitan counties had no provider (Henshaw et al., 1984).

A study of interstate variations in adolescent fertility in the United States found that residence in southern states was the most important predictor of high adolescent fertility (Morgan, 1983). The significance of region may reflect the facts that southern states spend less money on education and welfare and that abortion is less available in the South (Henshaw & Wallisch, 1984). AGI is currently sponsoring a study that will explore intercounty/interstate differences in greater detail.

These figures also reflect the size and age structure of the states as well as regional differences in reproductive behavior. However, the data are of interest in that they suggest that abortion providers in all states must be aware of any special needs of teenagers in the abortion process. Further, the large number of abortions to teenagers in the states identified suggests that targeting those states for special intervention programs would have substantial societal impact.

Length of Gestation

The length of gestation at which abortion is performed is a critical factor in evaluating the medical and psychological context of abortion. Both morbidity and mortality increase with length of gestation, even within each trimester (Tietze, 1983). Public policies and procedures that delay abortion thus compound risk to the health and well-being of the pregnant woman.

Younger women obtained abortions later in pregnancy than older women; the younger the teenager, the more likely the delay. For the 32 states reporting to the CDC in 1980, women under 19 years of age accounted for 29% of all abortions but accounted for more than 40% of abortions performed at more than 16 weeks of gestation. Of abortions obtained by adolescents aged 15 or less, 34% were performed at 8 weeks or earlier in gestation, compared with 41% among 15- to 19-year-olds and 51% among women aged 20–24. Adolescents below 15 years of age were twice as likely to have abortions at 16 weeks or later in gestation than were adolescents 15–19 years of age (14% vs. 7%). In contrast, only 4% of abortions to 20- to 24-year-olds were beyond 16 weeks of gestation. Note that the risk of death at 16 weeks of gestation is 13 times that at 8 weeks or less.

The most detailed data by age and gestation come from New York State (Tietze, 1983). As Figure 6 shows, by 25 years of age, 90% of abortions are performed before 12 weeks of gestation. The change in pattern reflects both an increased number of abortions performed below 8 weeks of gestation and a reduction of the number of abortions performed above 13 weeks of gestation.

Many factors affect length of gestation before abortion. Eight in 10 counties have no facilities for abortion. Travel distance, inability to confide in others, ignorance about the health care system, menstrual irregularity, inexperience in recognizing symptoms of pregnancy, and psychological factors, particularly the use of denial, can all contribute to delay in seeking abortion (AGI, 1981).

Parental notification requirements—or the belief that such requirements exist even when clinics do not have such a policy—may also contribute to delay in seeking abortion. More than 4 in 10 facilities have parental notification requirements for girls aged 15 or younger, and 3 in 10 require parental consent or notification for 17-year-olds. See the work of Melton and Pliner, and also Scott in this volume for discussion of the legal and ethical issues in abortion counseling of minors.

ABORTION COSTS

Length of gestation affects cost and access to clinic service providers as well. In 1981 the average clinic charge for a first-trimester

FIGURE 6

Percentage distribution of legal abortions by weeks of gestation and woman's age: New York State, 1980. From *Induced Abortion: A World Review, 1983* (5th ed.), by C. Tietze, 1983 (New York: Population Council).

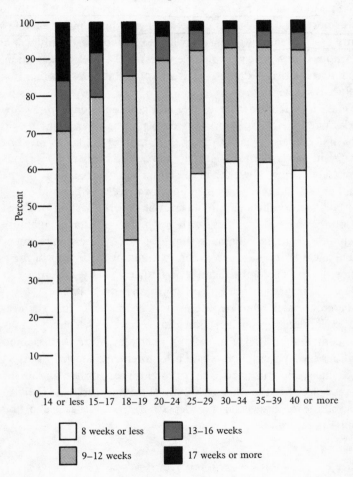

abortion was $190; the cost for a second-trimester dilation and evacuation (D&E) averaged $358. Since only 21% of clinics provide second-trimester services, teenagers who delay seeking abortions must have them in the more expensive hospital setting, where the average cost of a second-trimester D&E is $740 (Henshaw, 1982).

Cost continues to be an issue for teenagers; 9 in 10 teenagers aged 17 years or younger rely on their partners, parents, or Medicaid to defray the cost of an abortion. Again, age makes a difference. In 1979, for teens 15 years or younger, 2 out of 5 had abortions paid for by parents, one-fifth by partners, and one-fourth by Medicaid; one-tenth shared the cost with parents or partner; only 1 in 25 paid alone. Among older teenagers, a partner was more likely to pay than a parent, but even for 17-year-olds, only 1 in 10 young women paid for the abortion herself (AGI, 1981).

Costs may be especially burdensome for teenagers under age 15, who are more likely than older teenagers to be referred to a hospital for an abortion, even in the first trimester. One study of first-trimester abortions in 14 states found that 24.3% of abortions performed on adolescents under 15 years of age were done in hospitals compared with 14.6% of first-trimester abortions on 15- to 19-year-olds (Henshaw & O'Reilly, 1983).

MEDICAL OUTCOMES

It is well documented that in the United States the risk of dying from complications related to childbirth is about seven times the risk from having an abortion, combining all weeks of gestation (LeBolt, 1982). Tietze (1983) has shown that reliance on barrier methods of contraception, with early abortion as a backup method, is the safest reversible means of controlling fertility at any age.

Recent research suggests that teenagers have an even lower risk of death from abortion than women aged 20 years or older and have no higher risk of experiencing most of the complications associated with abortion, including fever of three or more days' duration, transfusion, and unintended surgery. Cervical injury is the only complication for which teenagers have a higher risk. From 1972 to 1978, the crude death-to-case rate for teenagers was 1.3 per 100,000 procedures. In contrast, the rate was 2.9 for women 30 and older. Death-to-case rates generally increased with the woman's age within each gestational period. Although abortions performed on teenagers are generally safer than those on older women, the finding of 5.5 cervical injuries per 1,000 procedures prompted researchers to suggest that more gradual dilation of the cervix may help reduce the rate of cervical injury (Cates, Schulz, & Grimes, 1983).

THE INTERNATIONAL PICTURE

Tietze (1983) provides a detailed overview of abortion laws and policies around the world. In 1982, 10% of the world's population lived in countries where abortion was totally prohibited, and 18% lived in countries where it was permitted only if the woman's life was endangered. Because of the differences in legal status and enforcement of abortion laws, interpretations of cross-cultural differences in abortion incidence must be made with caution.

An estimated 30 to 55 million abortions are performed worldwide each year. The United States ranks fifth among the 16 countries reporting abortion rates and sixth among those reporting abortion ratios (number of abortions/1,000 live births). The United States, Canada, and Scotland reported the highest percentage of abortions obtained by teenagers. About 30% of abortions in each of those countries were obtained by teenagers. The lowest percentages were reported in Czechoslovakia, Singapore, and Tunisia, where fewer than 10% of abortions were obtained by adolescents.

Table 2 shows the major role that abortion plays in fertility control for young women around the world, depicting legal abortions to teenagers for selected countries, by the latest available year. In general, both percentage of adolescent abortions and abortion rates per 1,000 women increased with age. Abortion ratios, however, generally declined, except for Hungary.

TABLE 2

Legal Abortions Obtained by Women under 20 Years of Age: Selected Areas, Latest Available Year

		Age of woman[a]		
Area	Year	Below 15 years	15–17 years	18–19 years

Percentage of abortions at all ages

Canada	1981	0.8	12.3	15.2
Czechoslovakia	1981	0.0	2.0	4.1
Denmark	1981	0.5	7.4	9.9
England and Wales[b]	1980	0.7	13.4	13.5
Finland	1980	0.3	10.3	13.5
France	1979	0.1	3.9	8.9
German Dem. Rep.	1976	0.1	6.4	7.0
German Fed. Rep.	1981	0.2	4.9	8.2
Hungary	1980	0.2	4.2	5.9
Netherlands[b]	1979	0.6	8.3	8.8
New Zealand	1981	0.5	10.6	13.2
Norway	1981	0.6	12.4	13.1
Sweden	1981	0.7	8.3	9.1
United States	1980	1.0	11.5	17.1

Abortion rates per 1,000 women[c]

Canada	1981	1.4	12.0	21.1
Czechoslovakia	1980	0.1	5.9	18.5
Denmark	1980	1.3	14.1	30.4
England and Wales[b]	1980	1.2	14.4	22.7
Finland	1980	0.6	13.8	27.1
German Dem. Rep.	1976	0.4	12.8	23.0
Hungary	1980	1.0	18.2	37.4
New Zealand	1981	0.6	8.1	14.7
Norway	1981	1.2	18.1	30.1

continued

TABLE 2, CONTINUED

Area	Year	Age of woman[a]		
		Below 15 years	15–17 years	18–19 years
Sweden	1980	2.0	16.3	29.6
United States	1980	4.3	30.2	61.0
Abortion rates per 100 known pregnancies[d]				
Canada	1980	46.5	38.2	27.5
Czechoslovakia	1980	24.5	19.7	12.4
England and Wales[b]	1979	60.6	38.4	23.2
German Dem. Rep.	1975	33.1	23.6	15.9
Hungary	1979	23.1	26.3	21.6
New Zealand	1979	23.2	16.1	7.9
Norway	1979	85.7	53.7	30.3
Sweden	1979	87.8	63.0	37.1
United States	1980	41.7	41.7	39.6

[a]Percentage and rates: age at termination. Ratios: age at conception.
[b]Residents only.
[c]Rates for abortions at below 15 years computed per 1,000 women aged 13–14 years.
[d]Legal abortions plus live births six months later.

SOURCE: *Induced Abortion: A World Review, 1983* (5th ed.), by C. Tietze, 1983 (New York: Population Council).

ABORTION IN CONTEXT: SEX, PREGNANCY, AND CHILDBIRTH

SEXUAL ACTIVITY HAS INCREASED

The rising rates of abortion since 1973 reflect a substantial rise in teenage sexual activity. By 1979 premarital sexual intercourse was not uncommon, with one out of two women aged 15–19 reporting they had ever had sexual intercourse. For women, the average age for initial intercourse was 16.2 years; for men the average was 15.7 years. Black women experienced intercourse at younger ages than whites. More than 36% of black females aged 15–19 had first experienced intercourse before age 15; the comparable figure for whites was 19% (Zelnik & Shah, 1983).

According to AGI (1984), in 1981, 42% of the nation's 27.6 million teenagers experienced sexual intercourse. Of these 11.6 million teenagers, 5 million were female. More than one out of five of these young women became pregnant; three out of four of those pregnancies were unintended.

Of the 5 million female adolescents at risk for unintended pregnancy in 1981 (i.e., who were sexually active, fecund, not surgically sterilized, not currently pregnant, and not trying to become pregnant), 52% were between 18 and 19 years of age; 43% were between ages 15 and 17; and 5% were below age 15.

Risk of unintended pregnancy changes markedly during adolescence. In 1981, for teenagers below age 15, only 3% of females were at risk. Between ages 15 and 17, the risk jumped to 37%. For ages 18–19, it increased to 63% (Torres & Forrest, 1983).

Although the risk of unintended pregnancy was substantial for all teenagers between ages 15 and 19, it was greater for poorer teenagers. For example, for 15- to 17-year-olds, more than 46% with family incomes below 150% of the poverty line, compared with 31% of such teenagers with family incomes greater than 250% of the poverty line, were at risk for unintended pregnancy (Torres & Forrest, 1983).

AGI (1983) also tells us that 4 of 10 of today's 20-year-old women have had at least one pregnancy during their teens; 2 out of 10 have given birth at least once; and more than 1 in 7 have had abortions.

We need to learn more about the factors that underlie the population statistics, including earlier physical maturation in adolescence, the availability of contraception, and the changing social and cultural values that increase the acceptability of teenage sexual activity and out-of-wedlock childbearing (cf. Shah & Zelnik, 1981; Thornton & Freedman, 1982).

CONTRACEPTIVE USAGE HAS INCREASED, BUT SUBSTANTIAL PROPORTIONS OF SEXUALLY ACTIVE TEENAGERS REMAIN UNPROTECTED

Although the proportion of unmarried teenage women engaging in sexual activity increased by two-thirds during the 1970s, pregnancies increased by only 12.5%, reflecting a substantial increase in the use of contraceptives by teenagers. The pregnancy rate of sexually active adolescents actually declined by 22%, while the contraceptive rate increased by 35%. Although there was a large increase in the number of abortions to teenagers from 1974 to 1979, there was a smaller increase in the number of abortions per 1,000 sexually active women (Baldwin, 1982).

As of 1979, among metropolitan area teenagers, 33% of unmarried white teenagers and 43% of unmarried black teenagers had conceived within 24 months of becoming sexually active (Koenig & Zelnik, 1982a). The months after initiation of sexual intercourse are a critical period for prevention of pregnancy (Zabin, Kantner, & Zelnik, 1979). Of all premarital pregnancies, 45% had been conceived within the first six months after initiation of sexual intercourse.

There is inconsistency between the sexual attitudes of adolescents and their behavior that is yet to be understood. One study of inner-city high-school juniors and seniors found that 83% of sexually experienced teenagers reported a best age for first intercourse that was older than their own age for first intercourse. More than one in three reported that they believed sexual intercourse before marriage was wrong, and even among the sexually experienced, one in four of both sexes reported that they believed premarital sex was wrong (Zabin, Hirsch, Smith, & Hardy, 1984).

PREGNANCY OUTCOME AND MARITAL STATUS IS RELATED TO EFFECTIVE USE OF CONTRACEPTION

Koenig and Zelnik (1982b) reported that unmarried teenagers whose first pregnancy ended in abortion were only half as likely to become pregnant a second time within 24 months as those unmarried teenagers whose first pregnancy resulted in a live birth. Although few unmarried teenagers who become pregnant marry during the pregnancy, those who do marry have a greater chance of becoming pregnant again within two years after the outcome of that pregnancy. This result appears to reflect less use, or less efficient use, of contraceptives.

In her analysis of data from the National Survey of Family Growth, Ford (1983) reported that the probability of a pregnancy during the year after a first birth for all teenage mothers was 17%. Second pregnancy rates were the same for whites and blacks. However, women with incomes below 150% of the poverty level had rates twice those of women above that level (21% vs. 11%).

It is important to note that even well-motivated teenagers who are conscientious about contraception may become pregnant. In one study (Westoff, DeLung, Goldman, & Forrest, 1981), one out of four adolescent abortion patients was using a contraceptive when she became pregnant, either because she did not use the method correctly or consistently or because the method itself failed to prevent pregnancy. Based on the data of that study, an estimated 10% of adolescents using contraception would be expected to become pregnant in a 12-month period.

CHILDBEARING BY UNMARRIED TEENAGERS IS OF PARTICULAR CONCERN

Since 1970, more than two out of three firstborn children of teenagers have been conceived out of wedlock; for black teenagers the proportion is 90% (O'Connell & Moore, 1980). In contrast, among women aged 20 and older, one out of two firstborns of black mothers and about 13% of firstborns of white mothers are conceived out of wedlock (O'Connell & Rogers, 1984).

The rise in births to unmarried teenagers, which lessened in the 1970s, compared with the previous decade, reflects the decreased likelihood that young women who choose to carry to term will marry to legitimize a birth. In 1981, 16% of unmarried pregnant teenagers married during the pregnancy, half the proportion of a decade earlier (Koenig & Zelnik, 1982b). During that year 267,828 babies were born to unmarried teenage mothers. Of that group, 118,608 (44.3%) were born to mothers aged 15–17; 8,859 babies (3.2%) were born to mothers aged 14 or under. A total of 128,844 (48.0%) were born to black mothers; 63,243 (49%) of that group were born to mothers under 17 years of age (Ventura, 1984).

From 1970 to 1981, the increase in nonmarital birth rates was much greater for white than for black teenagers (Figure 7). For whites, births increased 60% for teenagers aged 15–17 and 65% for teenagers aged 18–19; for blacks, births declined 1% for the younger group and increased 33% for the 18- to 19-year-olds (Ventura, 1984).

The impact of liberalization of abortion laws can be seen when comparing the rise in the rate of births to unmarried women in the 1960s and 1970s. In the 1960s the rate rose 34%. In the 1970s the rate rose 13%. After 1973 the rise came to a halt, but it began again in the late 1970s as fewer white teenagers married to legitimize births. Thus, birthrates to unmarried teenagers have fallen among nonwhites but not among whites (AGI, 1981).

ATTENTION TO ETHNIC AND CULTURAL ISSUES IS CRITICAL

These figures underscore the importance of considering ethnic and cultural issues in public policy discussions of reproductive choice. The efforts of policymakers who seek to curb access to abortion will have a greater impact on the lives of black teenagers. The political importance of having credible black leadership, particularly black female leadership, involved in policymaking cannot be understated.

SUMMARY AND FUTURE DIRECTIONS

Abortion plays a significant role in the control of adolescent fertility around the world. In the United States, that role is larger for

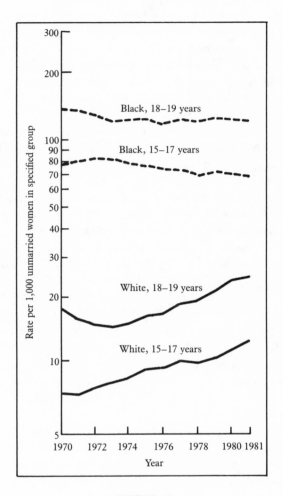

FIGURE 7

Birthrates for unmarried women aged 15–17 and 18–19 years, by race of child: United States, 1980–81. From "Trends in Teenage Childbearing, United States, 1970–81," by S. J. Ventura, in *Vital and Health Statistics*, Series 21, no. 41, Department of Health and Human Services Pub. No. (PHS) 84-1919 (Washington, DC: U.S. Government Printing Office).

younger teenagers, unmarried sexually active teenagers, and teenagers who are members of minority groups. Although abortion in the United States has been legal since 1973, there are still issues of access that are reflected in interstate variations in abortion rates and greater incidence of unwanted childbearing among poor women. Although mortality and morbidity associated with legal abortion are lower than those associated with childbirth, risks for teenagers are compounded by their greater tendency to delay seeking abortion. When length of gestation at abortion is controlled, however, teenagers have lower risks for death and for most complications than do older women.

The rising rates of sexual activity in early adolescence combined with less substantial gains in contraceptive protection means that many adolescents continue to be at substantial risk for unintended pregnancy, even in the early months after first initiation of intercourse. Given this situation, it is not surprising that abortion continues to play a substantial role in the control of adolescent fertility.

Policies aimed toward reducing the demand for abortion services must focus on the adolescent before first intercourse occurs. Occurrence of pregnancy is not necessary to motivate teenagers to use contraception. Indeed there is some evidence that teenagers who have never been pregnant are more likely than their peers who have been pregnant to return to a family planning clinic after their initial visit and to do so in a shorter time (Bernardik, Namerow, & Weinstein, 1982).

Although considerable attention has been paid to the relationships among social and biological factors, sexual behavior, and use of contraception (cf. Zelnik, Kantner, & Ford, 1981), there has been little movement beyond descriptive models toward examination of factors causally related to teenagers' reproductive events. Theory-based behavioral and psychological research is needed to develop those causal models, particularly basic research on motivation and on the relation between attitudes and behavior. There are major gaps between what adolescents believe and how they behave, and psychologists have yet to delineate adequately what contributes to the differences.

We need to know more about teenagers' sexual lives and their ability to assess the risks and benefits of sex, contraception, and childbearing. We need to know more about the social and cognitive development of teenagers in early, middle, and late adolescence, particularly with regard to the self-concept and self-esteem of young girls. Basic research in developmental processes as well as social and cultural conditions in adolescence is requisite for developing effective policies and programs aimed at avoiding teenage pregnancy.

Issues of access to family planning and abortion continue and may be expected to intensify as abortion opponents increase their political strength. The psychological impact of the bombings of abortion clinics on access also needs to be assessed. However, we must go beyond issues of access and examine the demand for abortion in the context of the roles and status of women.

We need to examine how sex role socialization contributes to the incidence of unintended pregnancy. Socializing females to be passive, to have low self-esteem, and to hold limited aspirations and creating sex-role expectations that emphasize male prerogatives and interfere with the mutual communication and respect needed for the development of nonexploitive sexual relationships have worked against avoidance of unwanted pregnancy (Russo, 1979, 1983). Can alternatives be generated?

We need to examine the real as well as the perceived opportunities for women at risk for teenage pregnancy, particularly for members of minority groups, and develop ways to motivate girls to define and work toward goals that are incompatible with unprotected sexual intercourse. The importance of this effort is seen in the small survey of 30 lower-class, predominantly black teenage mothers by Henderson (1980), who examined the discrepancy between the views of professionals and those of the teenagers themselves with regard to the consequences of childbirth.

Despite the data on negative outcomes of teenage motherhood, which were cited by the professionals and shaped the women's views, Henderson found that teenagers reported that having a child had not substantially changed their lives or their expectations for the future. As Henderson insightfully observed, "Greater difficulty in gaining employment, greater likelihood of using public assistance, and limited possibilities of extended educational activities will hardly be considered as consequences of early motherhood when unemployment and public assistance are commonplace and extended education is uncommon" (p. 82).

This discussion is only a profile of the psychosocial context of teenage abortion. A full picture must consider the context of adolescent pregnancy and childbearing, including factors associated with beginning and continuing sexual activity; preventing pregnancy or becoming pregnant; resolving an unintended pregnancy; and consequences of the means of pregnancy resolution: abortion, birth with adoption, and birth with keeping the child (cf. Chilman, 1980, 1983). Each of these stages has implications for public policy intervention at federal, state, and local levels. I hope that this brief overview will be a useful step toward constructing that full picture.

References

Alan Guttmacher Institute. (1981). *Factbook on teenage pregnancy. Tables and references for teenage pregnancy: The problem that hasn't gone away.* New York: Author.

Alan Guttmacher Institute (1982). *Teenage pregnancy: The problem that hasn't gone away.* New York: Author.

Alan Guttmacher Institute. (1983). School sex education in policy and practice, *Issues in Brief, 3,* 1–6.

Alan Guttmacher Institute. (1984). Toward a comprehensive approach: What government can do about teenage pregnancy. *Issues in Brief, 4,* 1–4.

Baldwin, W. (1982). Trends in adolescent contraception, pregnancy, and childbearing. In E. R. McAnarney (Ed.), *Premature adolescent pregnancy and parenthood.* New York: Grune and Stratton.

Bernardik, E., Namerow, P. B., & Weinstein, M. (1982). *Does a prior pregnancy affect choice of contraceptive method or effectiveness of use?* Paper presented at the annual meeting of the American Public Health Association, Montreal, November 14–18.

Cates, W., Jr., Schulz, K. F., & Grimes, D. A. (1983). The risks associated with teenage abortion. *New England Journal of Medicine, 309*, 621.

Center for Population Options. (1984). Hispanic community embraces "life planning." *Population Options, 4*, 1–2.

Centers for Disease Control. (1983). *Abortion surveillance, annual summary, 1979–1980.*

Chilman, C. S. (Ed.). (1980). *Adolescent pregnancy and childbearing: Findings from research.* NIH Publication no. 81-2077. Washington, DC: U.S. Government Printing Office.

Chilman, C. S. (Ed.). (1983). *Adolescent sexuality in a changing American society* (2nd ed.). New York: Wiley.

Ezzard, N. V., Cates, W., Jr., Kramer, D. G., & Tietze, C. (1982). Race-specific patterns of abortion use by American teenagers. *American Journal of Public Health, 72*, 809.

Ford, K. (1983). Second pregnancies among teenage mothers. *Family Planning Perspectives, 15*, 268–272.

Henderson, G. H. (1980). Consequences of school-age pregnancy and motherhood. *Family Relations, 29*, 185.

Henshaw, S. (1982). Freestanding abortion clinics: Services, structure, fees. *Family Planning Perspectives, 14*, 248–256.

Henshaw, S. K., Forrest, J. D., & Blaine, E. (1984). Abortion services in the United States, 1981 and 1982. *Family Planning Perspectives, 16*, 119–127.

Henshaw, S. K., & O'Reilly, K. (1983). Characteristics of abortion patients in the United States, 1979 and 1980. *Family Planning Perspectives, 15*, 5–15.

Henshaw, S. K., & Wallisch, L. S. (1984). The Medicaid cutoff and abortion services for the poor. *Family Planning Perspectives, 16*, 170–172, 177–180.

Koenig, M. A., & Zelnik, M. (1982a). The risk of premarital first pregnancy among metropolitan-area teenagers: 1976 and 1979. *Family Planning Perspectives, 14*, 239–247.

Koenig, M. A., and Zelnik, M. (1982b) Repeat pregnancies among metropolitan-area teenagers: 1971–1979. *Family Planning Perspectives, 14*, 341–344.

LeBolt, S. A. (1982). Mortality from abortion and childbirth. Are the populations comparable? *Journal of the American Medical Association, 248*, 188–191.

McCormick, M. C., Shapiro, S., & Starfield, B. (1984). High-risk young

Adolescent Abortion: The Epidemiological Context

mothers: Infant mortality and morbidity in four areas of the United States, 1973–1978. *American Journal of Public Health, 74,* 18.

Morgan, C. S. (1983). Interstate variations in teenage fertility. *Population Research and Policy Review, 2,* 67.

New York State Council on Children and Families. (1984). *Special report: Adolescent pregnancy,* June.

O'Connell, M., & Moore, M. J. (1980). The legitimacy status of first births to U.S. women aged 15–24, 1973–1978. *Family Planning Perspectives, 12,* 16–25.

O'Connell, M., & Rogers, C. C. (1984). Out-of-wedlock births, premarital pregnancies, and their effect on family formation and dissolution. *Family Planning Perspectives, 16,* 157–162.

Russo, N. F. (1983, June 28). *Psychological aspects of unintended pregnancy and abortion.* Statement to the Subcommittee on Health and the Environment, Committee on Energy and Commerce, United States House of Representatives.

Russo, N. F. (Ed.). (1979). The motherhood mandate. *Psychology of Women Quarterly, 4,* whole no. 1.

Shah, F., & Zelnik, M. (1981). Parent and peer influence on sexual behavior, contraceptive use, and pregnancy experience of young women. *Journal of Marriage and the Family, 43,* 339–348.

Thornton, A., & Freedman, D. (1982). Changing attitudes towards marriage and single life. *Family Planning Perspectives, 14,* 297–303.

Tietze, C. (1983). *Induced abortion: A world review, 1983.* (5th ed.). New York: Population Council.

Torres, A., & Forrest, J. D. (1983). Family planning clinic services in the United States, 1981. *Family Planning Perspectives, 15,* 272–278.

Ventura, S. J. (1984). Trends in teenage childbearing, United States, 1970–81. *Vital and health statistics,* series 21, no. 41. Department of Health and Human Services. Pub. no. (PHS) 84-1919. Washington, DC: U.S. Government Printing Office.

Westoff, C. F., Calot, G., & Foster, A. D. (1983). Teenage fertility in developed nations: 1971–1980. *Family Planning Perspectives, 15,* 105–110.

Westoff, C. F., DeLung, J. S., Goldman, N., & Forrest, J. D. (1981). Abortions preventable by contraceptive practice. *Family Planning Perspectives, 13,* 218–223.

Zabin, L. S., Hirsch, M. B., Smith, E. A., & Hardy, J. B. (1984). Adolescent sexual attitudes and behavior: Are they consistent? *Family Planning Perspectives, 16,* 181–185.

Zabin, L. S., Kantner, J. F., & Zelnik, M. (1979). The risk of adolescent pregnancy in the first months of intercourse. *Family Planning Perspectives, 11,* 215.

Zelnik, M., Kantner, J. F., & Ford, K. (1981). *Sex and pregnancy in adolescence.* Beverly Hills, CA: Sage.

Zelnik, M., & Shah, F. K. (1983). First intercourse among young Americans. *Family Planning Perspectives, 15,* 64–70.

NANCY E. ADLER AND PEGGY DOLCINI

Psychological Issues in Abortion for Adolescents

An unwanted pregnancy frequently creates a crisis for an adolescent female as well as for her partner, family, and caregivers. The young woman must make a decision that requires balancing medical, social, moral, religious, and interpersonal concerns. She may well be subjected to conflicting pressures to continue or terminate the pregnancy and must decide in a highly charged social context in which even her right to make such a choice is in question. There is no easy resolution to this crisis. As David (1972) has pointed out, "It may well be a truism that there is no psychologically painless way to cope with an unwanted pregnancy" (p. 61). A limited number of options are available, and each has its own set of problems.

Here we will consider the psychological issues involved in the alternative of abortion. It is beyond the scope of this chapter to consider the psychological issues involved in the creation of the pregnancy or in the other outcomes of carrying the baby to term and either keeping it or giving it up for adoption. All of these warrant chapters in themselves. We will consider two critical times in the abortion process, the decision-making phase preceding the procedure and the psychological aftereffects.

DECISION MAKING

The decision concerning the resolution of unwanted pregnancy is complex and stressful for most women. There are a number of stages in decision making, and each poses special problems for the adolescent. Several approaches have been taken to understanding this process. Brown (1983) applied the Beach and Mitchell decision-making model to the pregnancy resolution process in adolescents. Bracken, Klerman, and Bracken (1978a) developed a theoretical model of decision making regarding unwanted pregnancy based on the Janis and Mann (1977) model. The Bracken et al. model posits five stages. Although these may not universally occur in all women and in the order postulated, they provide a useful framework for examining the key issues in decision making and the special problems adolescents may encounter at each stage.

Stage One: Acknowledging Pregnancy

According to the model, the first stage begins with the last menstrual period and ends when a woman consciously acknowledges that she is pregnant. The length of this stage is crucial for several reasons. For the woman who continues her pregnancy, early acknowledgment increases the probability that she will obtain good prenatal care. For the woman who terminates her pregnancy, early acknowledgment allows time for adequate preparation for the abortion and makes possible procedures that are available only in the first trimester. Since second-trimester abortions are associated with greater physical and psychological problems than are first-trimester abortions (Kaltreider, 1973; Osofsky, Osofsky, Rajan, & Spitz, 1975), prompt action may contribute to a better outcome.

This first stage is likely to be longer for adolescents than for older women. Denial of pregnancy, uncertainty about whom to turn to, and fear of confronting parents are important factors in delay (Nadelson, 1974). Young adolescents are particularly likely to use denial about a possible pregnancy. Hatcher (1976) presented findings based on clinical experience and on an in-depth study of thirteen adolescents over the course of and following a pregnancy ending in abortion.[1] Hatcher found that young adolescents (under age 15) delayed longer than older adolescents in seeking medical advice and tended to attribute their pregnancy symptoms to other causes, such as the flu. She reported that "one adolescent insisted that she 'had a tumor' even when confronted with a positive pregnancy test" (p. 414). The defensive use of denial may be reinforced by the adolescent's belief that she is too young, too special, or too immature to become pregnant. Such beliefs are commonly voiced by young adolescents and may make it particularly difficult for them to consider the possibility that they are pregnant.

Even after the adolescent has realized and accepted that she is pregnant, there may be substantial delay before she acts to resolve the pregnancy. The younger the adolescent, the less experience she is likely to have had in seeking professional assistance. A young woman who does not want to involve her family or the family's doctor may not know where to turn for help. She may fear that a clinic or abortion provider will notify her parents and thus may put off seeking help. Clary (1982) found that a majority of minors obtaining abortions did not inform their parents. Without the usual supports, young people may not know where to go. Lewis (1981) found that, compared with older adolescents, younger people were less likely to think of the need for independent professional opinions even when indicated. In another study (Lewis, 1980), adolescents were found to be less likely than adults to expect to consult a professional regarding their pregnancies. Uncertainty about where to turn may lead to inaction. Further, in formulating options and carrying out a decision to terminate the pregnancy, an adolescent may become paralyzed by the complexity of the decisions involved and the fact that an abortion is irreversible (Brown, 1983). Indecision can be painful in itself, and many women have reported that the time between detection of pregnancy and the abortion was

---

1. Given the small sample size, Hatcher's conclusions must be taken as tentative. However, the richness of the data and of her clinical insight make her observations valuable.

more stressful than the postabortion period. At each of the stages described in the following pages there is the potential for delay as well as for impulsive action in order to reduce the discomfort of the state of indecision.

Stages Two and Three: Formulating and Weighing Options

The second and third stages, respectively, involve formulating alternatives and weighing their pros and cons. Only three possibilities are available to a pregnant woman: terminating the pregnancy, continuing it and keeping the child, or continuing it and relinquishing the child for adoption. Not all options will be considered. It appears that most women choosing abortion at least consider continuing the pregnancy. Women deciding to continue their pregnancies are relatively more likely *not* to have considered the alternatives (Steinhoff, 1978).

In formulating and considering options, adolescents may be affected by significant others. Unless the adolescent has been close to someone who has undergone an abortion, she is unlikely to know much about the procedure (Brown, 1983). The presence of role models, especially in the family, for one or another choice seems particularly important. Adolescents who choose abortion are more likely to report having a sister or other role model who has had an abortion than are those who carry to term; the latter are relatively more likely to report a role model who has had a child out of wedlock (Bracken et al., 1978a; Evans, Selstad, & Welcher, 1976).

The work of weighing options may contribute to a more successful outcome once a choice is made. By processing different considerations, a woman may be able to anticipate potential negative outcomes and may be less likely to experience regret or distress should they occur. Such anticipation may be difficult for younger adolescents, whose lack of cognitive development makes it more difficult to project themselves into the future and anticipate events (Lewis, 1981). In addition, Lewis (1980) found that, compared with adults, adolescents were more likely to see their decision as externally "compelled." In this sample, adolescents were as capable as older women of imagining the effects of different choices in their lives but were less likely to see these considerations as affecting their decisions.

The issues involved in decision making may differ by developmental stage. The concerns regarding the resolution of the pregnancy are generally tied to the reasons it occurred. The young adolescents studied by Hatcher (1976) found it difficult to imagine themselves as mothers. In fact, the motivation for pregnancy in some cases seems to have been to bring them closer to their own mothers. Consistent with the more frequent use of denial in the first stage of acknowledging pregnancy, they frequently denied responsibility for the pregnancy and its resolution. "Typically, the adolescent at this stage demands that somebody (preferably a mother substitute) rescue her from her plight; she lacks alternative options, should such a rescue not occur in accordance with her wishes" (Hatcher, 1976, p. 416). The resolution generally sought by those in the sample was abortion, for the desire was to eliminate the pregnancy. The young adolescent's desire to have an abortion herself was often coupled with a more negative and punitive social view that abortion is wrong for others. Such a disparity in views toward abortion for self and others is not unique to adolescents. Smetana (1978) found a disjunction between abstract judgments about abortion and women's views of their own abortion, and Freeman (1977) found that women's decisions regarding abortion often ran counter to their own attitudes.

Many adolescents are ambivalent during the decision-making process. Hatcher found middle adolescents (age 15 to 18) far more likely to exhibit ambivalence in this stage than either younger or older girls. While pregnancy in the younger adolescent was frequently related to a desire to become closer to her mother, in the middle adolescent it was more likely to relate to competition with the mother and a struggle for autonomy. The middle adolescents held two conflicting pictures: one a romantic, rosy picture of blissful motherhood and the other a frightening image of a demanding child that conflicted with their own dependency needs

78

(even if not acknowledged). Decision making for middle adolescents can become complicated when parents voice their wishes for one or another resolution, for these desires may become entangled in the daughter's struggle for autonomy.

Hatcher found that older adolescents (over age 18) were better able to anticipate the consequences of the different actions they might take. However, their greater awareness of the fetus made the choice for abortion somewhat more difficult. Despite this, the ability of older adolescents to anticipate the consequences of their action contributed to a more positive outcome.

Stage Four: Choice

The fourth stage represents commitment to one alternative. At this point the girl generally takes actions to implement her decision, such as making contact with an abortion clinic, adoption agency, or obstetrical clinic. Such steps are not necessary, of course, if she is involved in a health care system that provides contact and help in previous stages.

It appears that the younger the woman, the longer it takes her to see a physician when she suspects pregnancy. This delay may be related to conflict about the abortion: younger women may be more ambivalent about the abortion decision, and conflict in turn is related to delay in seeing a physician. As previously noted, inexperience in approaching professionals may also contribute to delay.

During the period of choice, a girl may selectively seek support from others, often informing only those people she expects to support the decision that she herself wants to make. In a sample of young, mostly black unmarried women, Bracken, Klerman, and Bracken (1978b) found that those who were deciding to deliver their babies discussed their decision with significantly more people than did those who were deciding to terminate their pregnancies. The former also reported receiving more support for their decision than did the latter. In a sample of white adolescents, one might find different patterns of support for birth and adoption.

Stage Five: Commitment

Once a decision is made, the girl enters the final stage insofar as she adheres to her decision even if faced with new, disconfirming information. Having reached a decision, she generally no longer wants to consider the pros and cons of the different alternatives. The length of this stage may vary with age. An early adolescent may quickly decide upon a resolution and be resistant to any counterarguments. In contrast, a middle adolescent's ambivalence may result in prolonged vacillation during which decisions are made and reversed. A late adolescent may be in an intermediate position, spending more time than a younger adolescent in weighing alternatives but being more able than a middle adolescent to maintain her commitment once a choice is made.

Common problems in making and implementing a choice derive from conflicting interests of the adolescent and her parents and/or partner, and from her own ambivalence. If a girl's parents are urging her to terminate her pregnancy, her resistance to abortion may be based partly on her desire for a child and partly on her desire to counter her parents' demands. In addition to conflicting concerns of parents and daughter, there may be differences between the desires of the young woman and her partner. In some instances she may want the baby but her partner may be pressuring her to terminate the pregnancy; in other cases the girl may not want to continue the pregnancy but may be urged to do so by her partner.

There is mixed evidence about how much influence parents, partner, and peers have. Early in the decision process adolescents may hesitate to involve their parents. Rosen (1980) reported that few adolescents told their parents when they first thought they were pregnant, turning instead to a girl friend or a male partner. After the pregnancy was confirmed, however, more than half involved their mothers in the decision regarding resolution of the pregnancy. Tendency to involve the mother was not associated with age but was associated with conflict over the decision: those who told their mothers reported greater conflict over the decision. The causal direction of this relationship is not clear; it is possible that teenagers who experienced greater conflict were more likely to turn to their mothers or that involvement of the mother generated more conflict. Lending some support to the former is the finding that those adolescents who chose an alternative that was more unusual for their peer group were more likely to seek their mothers' assistance: black adolescents choosing abortion and white adolescents choosing adoption sought their mothers' assistance more often than other groups.

Other studies have shown differences by age in the tendency to involve parents. Clary (1982) found that about a third of adolescents under 17 informed their parents and that the younger adolescents were more likely to do so. David and Rasmussen (1979) found older adolescents more likely to consult their partners rather than a parent than were younger adolescents. Ashton (1980) found that a greater proportion of women under 17 years of age talked to their mothers. However, though the younger adolescents were more likely to consult their mothers and also discussed their pregnancy with more people than did the older patients, they were less likely to fully discuss their concerns regarding their situation with those they did confide in than were women over 25 years old.

It is not clear how much adolescents are swayed by the desires of others. The study by Bracken et al. (1978b) described earlier suggested that adolescents were not heavily influenced by others' persuasion attempts. A somewhat different picture emerged from research by Eisen, Zellman, Leibowitz, Chow, and Evans (1983) examining variables that predict the choice an adolescent will make regarding pregnancy resolution. The teenagers were interviewed early in pregnancy, before either abortion or delivery. They were asked their perception of the opinions of significant others regarding the options open to them as well as their own opinion regarding each of the options. The pattern of responses suggested that the young women were affected in their choice by the views of others. Over a third of those who agreed that they should carry the pregnancy to term (and either remain single or marry) subsequently had abortions. In about three-quarters of these cases they also reported that one or more significant others (generally their mothers or partners) had strongly supported their having an abortion. The opinion of the teenagers' fathers was not related to the decision, but their girl friends' attitudes toward abortion were strongly associated with their own attitudes, which in turn were related to the choice of abortion. Also, as noted earlier, role models may provide support for one or another choice even if they do not directly persuade the young woman.

Encouraging Successful Decision Making

Given the conflicting pressures a pregnant adolescent may be subjected to and given potential lacks in cognitive development that may hinder effective decision making, the need for counseling pregnant teenagers is particularly great. It is considered the ethical responsibility of the health care provider to offer counseling that explores all the options available in any pregnancy (Brown, 1983). A statement by the American Academy of Pediatrics (1979) asserts that when abortion counseling is in conflict with the physician's (or other health care professional's) moral code, this should be explained to the patient. Nadelson (1974) notes the desirability of working with the family to avoid future unwanted pregnancies and to explore problems reflected by mutual acknowledgment of adolescent sexuality. Although the involvement of the parents and of the father of the child is encouraged (along with other supports such as clergy or social workers) by the American Academy of Pediatrics, there are conditions under which it may not be advisable to involve them. Families in which parents may be in an unstable psychological state may not be able to handle the additional stress of the young woman's pregnancy. In addition, severe cultural or religious opposition to abortion in some families may place a young woman who chooses to terminate a pregnancy (or just reveals a pregnancy) at risk of alienation from her family or even of physical violence.

Each patient should be given an opportunity to examine her decision with a neutral person. The provider who is counseling the patient needs to determine what the girl herself wants. To do this, one needs to explore motivational issues in the creation of the pregnancy and to find whether the patient has discussed her pregnancy with her parents and with her partner, what they want her to do, and what she herself would like to do.

Counseling should help the adolescent make the decision that is best for her. In so doing, she should be prepared for implementing her choice. For abortion patients, this includes preparation for the procedure itself. There is some anecdotal evidence from physicians who claim they can tell which patients have had counseling and which have not by how anxious and tense they are during the procedure. In addition, anticipation of physical, social, and emotional effects of abortion may help to reduce negative reactions to the experience. Marcus (1979) showed that counseling resulted in positive short-term effects, with patients reporting less depression and guilt and more relief if they had received counseling than if they had not. However, counseling did not seem to have long-term effects on contraceptive behavior. Both counseled and noncounseled patients became more effective contraceptors after the procedure. Although the counseled group demonstrated greater knowledge regarding contraception, there was no difference in incidence of repeat abortions in the following twelve months or in attendance at medical follow-ups.

Counseling may take a variety of forms. Bracken et al. (1973) compared the effectiveness of individual counseling and two types of group counseling. They found the approaches to be differentially effective for younger and older women, with younger patients finding the group counseling relatively more effective.

PSYCHOLOGICAL EFFECTS OF ABORTION

Although there is a good deal of research on social and economic effects of adolescent pregnancy (see Marecek, this volume), there are few studies that specifically focus on psychological sequelae for this age group. Most of the research has been either on adult women or on mixed samples in which adolescents have not been examined separately. In this section we will review what is known about psychological responses for women in general and consider how the reactions of adolescents may differ from those of their older counterparts.

Abortion is a stressful experience, but most studies have found it is not likely to lead to severe emotional distress, particularly in women who do not have preexisting problems. Olson (1980), in her review of the research literature, concluded that for the adolescent abortion "is neither psychologically harmful nor in other ways damaging to the patient" (p. 440). The predominant response following abortion is generally relief (Adler, 1975; Ewing & Rouse, 1973; Monsour & Stewart, 1973; Simon, Senturia, & Rothman, 1967). Women do experience periods of regret, depression, and guilt following the procedure, but they usually are mild and diminish rapidly over time and general functioning is not adversely affected (Cvejic, Lipper, Kinch, & Benjamin, 1977; Ford, Castelnuovo-Tedesco, & Long, 1971; Peck & Marcus, 1966; Smith, 1973).

For women with a previous psychiatric history, unwanted pregnancy, whether resolved by abortion or by term delivery, may be associated with an exacerbation of problems. Although they are rare, cases have been reported of women's experiencing psychotic breaks following abortion despite the absence of preexisting psychological problems (Spaulding & Cavenar, 1978). In light of statistics showing that suicide is the third leading cause of death among adolescents, one needs to be alert to this risk. Tishler (1981) reported two cases of adolescent females, both with prior suicide attempts, who attempted suicide following abortion. Those attempts occurred about the time the fetuses would have been delivered had they been carried to term.

FACTORS AFFECTING ADOLESCENTS' RESPONSE TO ABORTION

Compared with adults, adolescents appear to have somewhat more negative responses on average following abortion. Several studies have found an association between age and psychological effects (Adler, 1975; Bracken, Hachamovitch, & Grossman, 1974; Margolis, Davison, Hanson, Loos, & Mikkelsen, 1971; Payne, Kravitz, Notman, & Anderson, 1976). Although statistically significant, the magnitude of the differences is not generally great, and the negative reactions of adolescents are still generally mild. A number of factors may contribute to the *comparatively* more negative response of adolescents.

Developmental Stage

The dynamics involved in the creation of a pregnancy and its resolution may be affected by the developmental stage of the adolescent. In Hatcher's (1976) sample, older adolescents, who were more realistic about the pregnancy and its termination, showed the most positive responses to the procedure. Having anticipated some of the sense of loss, they showed less severe postabortion reactions and frequently felt matured by the experience. In contrast, early adolescents dealt with both the pregnancy and its termination by using denial. This group was the most difficult to follow after the abortion, providing indirect evidence that denial extended into the postabortion period. Middle adolescents were less able than the older patients to anticipate their reactions. They experienced more postabortion depression than they had expected. On later follow-up they reported being disappointed that they had not achieved independence from parents through their pregnancy and that their parents had not changed.

Delay

As we noted earlier, the pregnant adolescent is more likely to present later in pregnancy owing to problems of delay and lack of access. Since there is then less time available for decision making, the adolescent may feel more pressure to go ahead with an abortion even if she is still ambivalent. Issues that are unresolved before the abortion may then create more difficulties afterward. A second result of delayed contact is that the adolescent is likely to undergo the more stressful abortion procedures performed in the second trimester. The second-trimester procedures generally are performed after quickening, when the patient has already experienced fetal movement. It appears that patients who have the midtrimester procedures feel a greater sense of loss than do women having abortions earlier in pregnancy (Bracken et al., 1974; Kaltreider, 1973; Osofsky et al., 1975).

For patients undergoing second-trimester procedures, denial may be used as an aid to coping. On the basis of thirty patients who were followed after second-trimester abortions, Brewer (1978) concluded that the emotional consequences of the procedure are less negative than has been suggested and that denial is probably widely used and not inappropriate. Brewer reported one patient who, three months after a second-trimester abortion, denied ever feeling movement of the fetus, even though at the time of the abortion she was quite sure she had. It should be noted that even within the second trimester, the type of procedure performed affects the patient's response regardless of age. Patients show fewer negative psychological responses following midtrimester dilation and curettage than following saline induction (Kaltreider, Goldsmith, & Margolis, 1979; Osofsky et al., 1975).

Fantasies about the Child

Related to the timing of the procedure is the experience of active fantasies about the child. Inhibiting fantasies about the potential child appears to contribute to the successful resolution of the abortion experience (Senay, 1970). Wallerstein, Kurtz, and Bar-Din (1972) found that both the content and the intensity of fantasies about the child at the time young women were deciding about terminating their pregnancies related to difficulties after termination. Related to this is a finding by Smith (1973) that although most women showed positive responses to abortion, there were a small number who did not. These tended to be teenagers who, among other things, reported being particularly fond of children.

Fantasies about the potential child are obviously more likely to occur in the second trimester than earlier in pregnancy. Kaltreider (1973) found that midtrimester patients more often talked about their babies, whereas first-trimester patients referred to "this pregnancy" or "my condition." Teenagers, who are more likely to delay into the second trimester, may thus be more likely to experience such fantasies before abortion.

Social Support

The actual or anticipated responses of other people are important contributors to postabortion responses. Perceived support from significant others was reported by Moseley, Follingstead, Harley, and Heckel (1981) to be the single most important determinant of psychological reaction to abortion. Opposition to the decision to abort resulted in higher levels of anxiety, depression, and hostility; support from one significant other, however, balanced opposition from another.

Bracken et al. (1974) examined social support provided by parents and partners. When parents did not know about the abortion, a woman's estimate of their anticipated reaction was used. For women over 23 years of age, postabortion responses were most highly related to their partners' approval. Among younger women, parental support was relatively more important. Bracken et al. (1978a) found among a sample of never-married women that those who continued their pregnancy as well as those who terminated it found their decision easier and were more likely to accept and be satisfied with their choice if significant others supported the decision.

Support of the physician may also be important. Over half (62%) of the abortion patients studied by Greenglass (1975) thought their physicians' attitudes toward them were positive, while only 23% considered them negative and 13% said they were neutral. Scores on a personality inventory following the abortion were related to these perceptions; women who thought their physicians' attitudes were positive had more favorable scores on a number of scales. Treatment by other health care workers can also affect abortion patients' reactions to the procedure (Evans & Gusdon, 1973; Marder, 1970; Walter, 1970).

Relationship with Mother

In terms of social support, the most important person is likely to be the adolescent's mother. In a sample of abortion patients of all ages, Payne et al. (1976) found a history of a negative relationship with the mother to be associated with difficulty in working through the conflicts of unwanted pregnancy and abortion. The relationship with the mother may be particularly important for adolescents. Schaffer and Pine (1972) identified the central conflict in a sample of adolescent girls undergoing abortion as "between the wish to be mothered (the passive longings for the mother-of-infancy) and the urge to be mothering (with a sense of mastery, of making amends, and of renewal of self)" (p. 514). The resolution of this conflict was closely associated with the psychological outcome of the abortion. Those girls who identified more with the former motivation tended to become passive, letting their mothers take charge, and to establish regressive ties with their mothers. Those who identified with the mothering role were more able to care for themselves and coped more successfully with the abortion.

Coercion

Adolescents who want to have an abortion but who expect negative responses from others have problems of social support. The opposite problem is faced by adolescents who want to continue their pregnancies but who are pressured into terminating them. Negative responses to abortion are more likely when the adolescent has not been actively involved in the decision making (Wallerstein et al., 1972), does not feel that abortion is her first choice (Evans et al., 1976), or feels pressured into the decision by parents, peers, or partner (Senay, 1970). Pregnancy counseling should help the girl participate more fully in the decision. Those who do choose abortion are less likely to have regrets afterward and may be less likely to become pregnant again.

Religious and Ethnic Group

Payne et al. (1976) found that membership in a religious or ethnic group that is opposed to abortion was associated with difficulty with abortion. Some studies have found that Catholic patients feel more guilt after abortion than non-Catholics, while other studies have found no difference by religion but have found that patients who are more actively involved in their religion show more negative postabortion responses (Adler, 1975; Osofsky & Osofsky, 1972). Evans et al. (1976) found that those adolescent abortion patients who later regretted their decisions were likely to be younger than the others, to have parents with less education, to be Mexican-American, and to have done more poorly in school than those who were more satisfied with their choice.

THE ADOLESCENT MALE

There is increasing interest in the rights and responsibilities of the male partner regarding the outcome of pregnancy. Little is known about the effects an abortion has on the young male involved. Rothstein (1977) studied a group of young men who accompanied young women to a clinic for an abortion. These men, who constituted a minority of the partners, felt a shared responsibility for the unwanted pregnancy and wanted to participate actively in coping with the abortion. They perceived participation in the procedure as being important to their coping with its effects. Wallerstein and Bar-Din (1972) showed how an abortion affected both partners in terms of both their individual reactions and their functioning as a couple.

There appear to be significant differences in attitudes toward abortion between black and white adolescent males. Vadies and Hale (1977) reported on a study of more than 1,000 males, finding that the large majority of blacks were opposed to abortion on moral grounds and would not want their partner to have an abortion, whereas white males expressed the opposite attitude on both issues.

The attitudes, desires, and reactions of the male partner are largely unknown to researchers and health care providers. Many clinics exclude them. However, these issues are important in and of themselves and also because they contribute to the reactions of the women undergoing the procedure.

COMPARISON WITH COMPLETION OF PREGNANCY

The factors discussed above contribute to the risk of negative responses among women undergoing abortion. However, it must be kept in mind that the alternatives to abortion carry risks of their own. Athanasiou, Oppel, Michelson, Unger, and Yager (1973) compared women who were matched on various socioeconomic and demographic variables and who underwent early abortion, late abortion, or term delivery, concluding that "induced abortion appears to be a benign procedure compared to term birth, psychologically and physically" (p. 231). Similar findings are reported by Burnell et al. (cited in Osofsky et al., 1975), who compared abortion patients with women who relinquished their infants for adoption and with women having term deliveries resulting from wanted pregnancies. Both groups with unwanted pregnancies (abortion and adoption) had more severe psychological problems during pregnancy than did the group delivering wanted babies. At follow-up, the abortion group showed better adjustment and felt less negative about their experience than did the women who had given up their babies for adoption. In a sample of black, unmarried women aged 15 to 23, Graves (1975) found no significant differences in responses to the abortion versus the childbearing experience. In contrast, in a study of psychiatric admissions among Danish women, David, Rasmussen, and Holst (1981) reported higher rates of admission to psychiatric hospitals for women after abortion than for women carrying to term, although this did not control for the wantedness of the pregnancy.

Psychological Issues in Abortion for Adolescents

SUCCESSFUL AND UNSUCCESSFUL RESOLUTION

The experience of an unwanted pregnancy creates a psychosocial crisis for most young women. However, for those adolescents who have adequate coping abilities and a supportive environment, the experience can actually contribute to development. A large majority of teens interviewed two years after an abortion reported that the experience had matured them (Cvejic et al., 1977).

Most abortion patients exhibit improved contraceptive practice following abortion. Evans et al. (1976) compared the contraceptive practices of teenagers after abortion, term birth, or a negative pregnancy test. They found that more than 95% of those who had been pregnant were using contraception six months later, compared with only 59% of teenagers who had not been pregnant. Margolis, Rindfuss, Coghlan, and Rochat (1974) also found marked improvement in contraceptive practice following abortion. Among teenagers who had an abortion, 56% had never used a contraceptive before they became pregnant. Six months after the abortion, 88% were using some method. It is interesting that improvement was more marked for adolescent abortion patients than for adults. Cvejic et al. (1977) report similar findings concerning contraceptive use two years after an abortion. However, improvement may not persist. Schneider and Thompson (1976) found that contraceptive use was greatest immediately following an abortion and diminished over time. Its effectiveness after abortion is influenced by the same factors that affect its use beforehand. In addition, the motivation to avoid pregnancy is likely to be influenced by the young woman's experience with the resolution of her pregnancy. Those who feel that they freely chose to terminate, who were able to identify with an adult figure in the process, and who were matured by the experience are at lower risk of another pregnancy.

CONCLUSIONS

Although abortion is stressful for any woman, it generally does not pose a substantial threat to emotional well-being. Adolescents may be at somewhat greater risk than older women for difficulties while making a decision and in response to the procedure. At the same time, the experience has the potential to contribute to a young woman's growth and development. The likelihood of a favorable outcome will be enhanced if she participates actively in making the decision. This in turn requires services that are accessible and that reach her relatively early. Ideally, the family and partner of the young woman will be involved and will support her decision. In the many cases when the ideal is not achieved, service providers need to be particularly sensitive to the young woman's need for support, taking the opportunity to help her sort out the conflicting pressures and determine what is best for her.

REFERENCES

Adler, N. (1975). Emotional responses of women following therapeutic abortion. *American Journal of Orthopsychiatry, 45*, 446–456.

American Academy of Pediatrics. (1979). Pregnancy and abortion counseling. *Pediatrics, 63*, 920–921.

Ashton, J. R. (1980). Patterns of discussion and decision-making amongst abortion patients. *Journal of Biosocial Science, 12*, 247–259.

Athanasiou, R., Oppel, W., Michelson, L., Unger, I., & Yager, M. (1973). Psychiatric sequelae to term birth and induced early and later abortion: A longitudinal study. *Family Planning Perspectives, 5*, 227–231.

Bracken, M., Grossman, G., Hachamovitch, M., Sussman, D., & Schrieir, D. (1973). Abortion counseling: An experimental study of three techniques. *American Journal of Obstetrics and Gynecology, 117*, 10–19.

Bracken, M., Hachamovitch, M., & Grossman, A. (1974). The decision to abort and psychological sequelae. *Journal of Nervous and Mental Disorders, 15*, 155–161.

Bracken, M., Klerman, L., & Bracken, M. (1978a). Abortion, adoption, and motherhood: An empirical study of decision-making during pregnancy. *American Journal of Obstetrics and Gynecology, 130*, 251–262.

Bracken, M., Klerman, L., & Bracken, M. (1978b). Coping with pregnancy resolution among never-married women. *American Journal of Orthopsychiatry, 48*, 320–333.

Brewer, C. (1978). Induced abortion after feeling fetal movements: Its causes and emotional consequences. *Journal of Biosocial Science, 10,* 203–208.

Brown, M. A. (1983). Adolescents and abortion: A theoretical framework for decision-making. *Journal of Gynecological Nursing, 12,* 241–247.

Clary, F. (1982). Minor women obtaining abortions: A study of parental notification in a metropolitan area. *American Journal of Public Health, 72,* 283–285.

Cvejic, H., Lipper, I., Kinch, R. A., & Benjamin, P. (1977). Follow-up of 50 adolescent girls two years after abortion. *Canadian Medical Association Journal, 116,* 44–46.

David, H. P. (1972). Abortion in psychological perspective. *American Journal of Orthopsychiatry, 42,* 61–68.

David, H. P., & Rasmussen, N. K. (1979). *Resolution of adolescent pregnancy: Danish experience.* Paper presented to the American Psychological Association, New York.

David, H. P., Rasmussen, N. K., & Holst, E. (1981). Postpartum and postabortion psychotic reactions. *Family Planning Perspectives, 13,* 88–92.

Eisen, M., Zellman, G. L., Leibowitz, A., Chow, W. K., & Evans, J. R. (1983). Factors discriminating pregnancy resolution decisions of unmarried adolescents. *Genetic Psychology Monographs, 108,* 69–95.

Evans, D. A., & Gusdon, J. P. (1973). Postabortion attitudes. *North Carolina Medical Journal, 34,* 271–273.

Evans, J., Selstad, G., & Welcher, W. (1976). Teenagers: Fertility control behavior and attitudes before and after abortion, childbearing, or negative pregnancy test. *Family Planning Perspectives, 8,* 192–200.

Ewing, J. A., & Rouse, B. A. (1973). Therapeutic abortion and a prior psychiatric history. *American Journal of Psychiatry, 130,* 37–40.

Ford, C., Castelnuovo-Tedesco, P., & Long, K. (1971). Abortion: Is it a therapeutic procedure in psychiatry? *Journal of the American Medical Association, 218,* 1173.

Freeman, E. (1977). Influence of personality attributes on abortion experiences. *American Journal of Orthopsychiatry, 47,* 503–513.

Graves, W. L. (1975). *Sequelae of unwanted pregnancy: A comparison of unmarried abortion and maternity patients.* Unpublished master's thesis, Emory University School of Medicine, Atlanta.

Greenglass, E. R. (1975). Therapeutic abortion and its psychological implications: The Canadian experience. *CMA Journal, 113,* 754–757.

Hatcher, S. (1976). Understanding adolescent pregnancy and abortion. *Primary Care, 3*, 407–425.

Janis, I. L., & Mann, L. (1977). *Decision making.* New York: Free Press.

Kaltreider, N. (1973). Emotional patterns related to delay in decision to seek legal abortion: A pilot study. *California Medicine, 118*, 23–27.

Kaltreider, N., Goldsmith, S., & Margolis, A. (1979). The impact of midtrimester abortion techniques on patients and staff. *American Journal of Obstetrics and Gynecology, 135*, 235–238.

Lewis, C. C. (1980). A comparison of minors' and adults' pregnancy decisions. *American Journal of Orthopsychiatry, 50*, 446–453.

Lewis, C. C. (1981). How adolescents approach decisions: Changes over grades seven to twelve and policy implications. *Child Development, 52*, 538–544.

Marcus, R. J. (1979). Evaluating abortion counseling. *Dimensions in Health Service, 56*, 16–19.

Marder, L. (1970). Psychiatric experience with a liberalized abortion law. *American Journal of Psychiatry, 126*, 1230–1236.

Margolis, A. J., Davison, L. A., Hanson, K. H., Loos, S. A., & Mikkelsen, C. A. (1971). Therapeutic abortion: Follow-up study. *American Journal of Obstetrical Gynecology, 110*, 243–249.

Margolis, A., Rindfuss, R., Coghlan, P., & Rochat, R. (1974). Contraception after abortion. *Family Planning Perspectives, 6*, 56–60.

Monsour, K., & Stewart, B. (1973). Abortion and sexual behavior in college women. *American Journal of Orthopsychiatry, 43*, 803–814.

Moseley, D. T., Follingstead, D. R., Harley, H., & Heckel, R. V. (1981). Psychological factors that predict reaction to abortion. *Journal of Clinical Psychology, 37*, 276–279.

Nadelson, C. (1974). Abortion counseling: Focus on adolescent pregnancy. *Pediatrics, 54*, 765–769.

Olson, L. (1980). Social and psychological correlates of pregnancy resolution among adolescent women: A review. *American Journal of Orthopsychiatry, 50*, 432–445.

Osofsky, J. D., & Osofsky, H. J. (1972). The psychological reaction of patients to legalized abortion. *American Journal of Orthopsychiatry, 42*, 48–60.

Osofsky, J. D., Osofsky, H. J., Rajan, R., & Spitz, D. (1975). Psychosocial aspects of abortion in the United States. *Mount Sinai Journal of Medicine, 42*, 456–467.

Payne, E. C., Kravitz, A. R., Notman, M. T., & Anderson, J. V. (1976).

Outcome following therapeutic abortion. *Archives of General Psychiatry, 33,* 725–733.

Peck, A., & Marcus, H. (1966). Psychiatric sequelae of therapeutic interruption of pregnancy. *J. of Nervous and Mental Diseases, 143,* 417–425.

Rosen, R. H. (1980). Adolescent pregnancy decision-making: Are parents important? *Adolescence, 15,* 43–54.

Rothstein, A. A. (1977). Men's reactions to their partners' elective abortions. *American Journal of Obstetrics and Gynecology, 128,* 831–837.

Schaffer, C., & Pine, F. (1972). Pregnancy, abortion, and the developmental tasks of adolescence. *Journal of the American Academy of Child Psychiatry, 11,* 511–536.

Schneider, A. M., & Thompson, D. J. (1976). Repeat aborters. *American Journal of Obstetrics and Gynecology, 126,* 316–320.

Senay, E. C. (1970). Therapeutic abortion: Clinical aspects. *Archives of General Psychiatry, 23,* 408–415.

Simon, N., Senturia, A., & Rothman, D. (1967). Psychiatric illness following therapeutic abortion. *Am. J. of Psychiatry, 124,* 97–103.

Smetana, J. (1978). *Relationships between abortion decisions and beliefs about the permissibility of abortion.* Paper presented to the American Psychological Association, Toronto.

Smith, E. M. (1973). A follow-up study of women who request abortion. *American Journal of Orthopsychiatry, 43,* 574–585.

Spaulding, J. G., & Cavenar, J. O. (1978). Psychoses following therapeutic abortion. *American Journal of Psychiatry, 135,* 364–365.

Steinhoff, P. G. (1978). Premarital pregnancy and the first birth. In W. B. Miller and L. F. Newman (Eds.), *The first child and family formation,* 180–208. Chapel Hill, NC: Carolina Population Center.

Tishler, C. L. (1981). Adolescent suicide attempts following elective abortion: A special case of anniversary reaction. *Pediatrics, 68,* 670–671.

Vadies, E., & Hale, D. (1977). Attitudes of adolescent males toward abortion, contraception, and sexuality. *Social Work in Health Care, 3,* 169–174.

Wallerstein, J. & Bar-Din, M. (1972). Seesaw response of a young married couple to therapeutic abortion. *Arch. of Gen. Psychiatry, 27,* 251–254.

Wallerstein, J., Kurtz, P., & Bar-Din, M. (1972). Psychosocial sequelae of therapeutic abortion in young unmarried women. *Arch. of Gen. Psychiatry, 27,* 828–832.

Walter, George S. (1970). Psychologic and emotional consequences of elective abortion. *Obstetrics & Gynecology, 36,* 482–491.

JEANNE MARECEK

Consequences of Adolescent Childbearing and Abortion

With roughly a million teenagers getting pregnant each year, the United States has the highest rate of adolescent pregnancy of any developed nation. Of these million teenagers, about 600,000 give birth (Zero Population Growth, 1977). The consequences of such early pregnancies and births are serious and often long lasting. Thus the question of avenues of recourse has important implications not only for the teenagers themselves and for their families but also for society.

This chapter summarizes the research on the social, psychological, and economic consequences of adolescent childbearing and abortion. The consequences of adolescent childbearing reviewed here include not only those experienced by the pregnant teenager herself but also those that affect her family of origin, the child, and the father of the child, as well as society at large. Next I survey the consequences of ending a pregnancy by induced abortion. For both adolescent childbearing and adolescent abortion, I consider beneficial outcomes as well as those that are disadvantageous.

Policies on adolescent abortion must be informed by an understanding of the context in which teenagers bear children. Thus, before reviewing the consequences of adolescent childbearing and abortion, I will present some statistics on the incidence and management of teenage pregnancy and childbirth.

The vast majority of teenagers who give birth are 15 years of age or older. Nonetheless, roughly 30,000 girls who are younger than 15 give birth each year, and this is on the increase (Baldwin, 1978). About 60% of teenage pregnancies result in live births, 30% are terminated by induced abortions, and the remaining 10% end in miscarriages or spontaneous abortions (Zero Population Growth, 1977).

Most pregnancies among teenagers appear to be unintended. Using data from a national survey, Zelnik, Kantner, and Ford (1981) estimated that 68% of premarital pregnancies among teenagers are "unwanted." Similarly, in a study of first pregnancies among lower-income black teenagers, Flaherty and her colleagues found that 66% of the pregnant girls said that they had not expected to get pregnant (Flaherty, Marecek, Olsen, & Wilcove, 1982). Unintended pregnancies, whether due to carelessness or to ignorance, inflict considerable disruption and psychological stress on the teenage couple and their families.

As might be expected, most teenage pregnancies are conceived out of wedlock, but about half of teenage mothers are married at the time of birth. There is a considerable difference between black and white teenagers in their rates of out-of-wedlock childbearing. According to the 1980 census, 85% of births to black teenagers were out of wedlock compared with 33% of births to white teenagers. Part of this disparity is because white girls are more likely to marry after a premarital conception (Zelnik et al., 1981).

Although girls from any socioeconomic or ethnic background can become pregnant, black teenagers and teenagers from lower socioeconomic groups are at higher risk for bearing children than are white teenagers or those who are more affluent. The racial disparity is especially prominent in younger cohorts of teenagers. Among girls aged 10–14, the birthrate for nonwhites is five times as high as it is for whites. Among 19-year-olds, however, it is less than twice as high (Baldwin, 1978). The higher birthrate among black teenagers is the result of many factors: black teenagers are more likely than white teenagers to be sexually active; those who are sexually active are more likely to get pregnant; and those who get pregnant are more likely to carry the pregnancy to term than are white teenagers (Zelnik et al., 1981). Because black communities and low-income communities will be more broadly affected by policies on adolescent fertility, policy discussions need to be sensitive to the norms and special interests of these groups.

The careful reader may notice that in the discussion that follows the option of giving a child up for adoption is not mentioned. Rather, the consequences of having an abortion are contrasted with the consequences of bearing a child *and raising it*. In theory, adoption is a third means of resolving a problem pregnancy. It is frequently proposed as the solution to the moral dilemma that abortion may pose. But at present few teenagers choose to place their babies for adoption (Zelnik et al., 1981). Moreover, there are very few studies of the consequences of adoption for the biological parents, the adoptive parents, or the adopted child. Hence the discussion of adoption will not be taken up here.

THE CONSEQUENCES OF ADOLESCENT CHILDBEARING

CONSEQUENCES TO TEENAGE MOTHERS

Bearing a child, whether in or out of wedlock, often has severe and protracted consequences for a teenager. Indeed, if she keeps the child, most areas of her life will be affected—her education, her occupational attainment, her economic well-being, and her subsequent marital and childbearing experiences.

Educational Attainment

A pregnancy that is carried to term usually causes some disruption in a teenager's schooling. Though girls have the legal right to remain in school throughout a pregnancy and to return after giving birth, there are a number of practical and emotional barriers to doing so. For example, many girls interviewed by Flaherty et al. felt obligated to care for their infants themselves; others had doubts about leaving their child with a paid caretaker (Flaherty et al., 1982). Moreover, even if a girl wished to place her child in day care, the severe shortage of facilities for infants and the high cost of child-care services make it unlikely that she could afford to do so (cf. Kamerman, 1979). Moreover, disapproval, hostility, or ridicule by school personnel or students may make a girl reluctant to continue school when her pregnancy becomes visible or to return after giving birth.

A number of studies have demonstrated that giving birth as a teenager is likely to have relatively permanent effects on a woman's educational attainment. For example, two studies that followed adolescent childbearers into their twenties found that their educational attainment remained below that of their counterparts who delayed childbearing (Card, 1977; Marecek, 1979). Card's study showed that this remained true even when such antecedent variables as socioeconomic status, intellectual interests, and educational aspirations before the pregnancy were statistically controlled.

The data further suggest that the negative effects on educational attainment are more severe for white than for black teenagers (Card, 1977; Moore & Waite, 1977). There are two possible reasons for this. First, because of the frequency of adolescent childbearing in the black community, there may be better supports for adolescent mothers in their families, schools, and neighborhoods. These supports may enable them to continue their schooling. The second reason is that norms in the white community more strongly sanction illegitimate births. Thus, white adolescents who get pregnant may be compelled into early marriages that preclude their return to school.

Occupational Attainment

As might be expected, early childbearing is associated with subsequent lower economic status. This has been demonstrated using a number of different indexes including employment history, occupational status, household income, and welfare dependency. For example, Marecek (1979) found that during the first seven years following the birth of the child, teenage mothers worked less of the time than their counterparts who delayed giving birth until their twenties. Card (1977) and Marecek (1979) found that the jobs teenage mothers held when they were in their twenties were lower in status than those of women who delayed childbearing. The diminished educational attainment of teenage childbearers is an important reason for their subsequent low occupational attainment (McLaughlin, 1977). Additional reasons include the larger family sizes of women who begin childbearing in their teens and their greater likelihood of heading single-adult households.

Economic Status

Given their more limited employment history and their lower occupational status, it is not surprising that teenage mothers also report lower household incomes (Card, 1977; Marecek, 1979). For example, Card examined reports of income when such women were 19, 23, and 29 years of age. At all three points, their incomes were lower than those of a matched group who delayed childbearing.

Adolescent mothers are also more likely to be receiving public assistance. Presser (1975) found that 68% of teenage mothers living in New York City lived in households receiving welfare. Marecek (1979) found that, in an inner-city sample, the likelihood of being on welfare seven years after the birth of the child was strongly related to age at first birth. Of women who gave birth before they were 15 years old, 46% were on public assistance, as were 28% of those who gave birth between the ages of 15 and 17 and 14% of those who gave birth at 18 or 19 years old. Only 3% of a comparison group who delayed childbearing until they were 20–25 years of age were on public assistance.

Marital Experiences

As one might expect, an early pregnancy often influences a young woman's subsequent marital experiences. In some cases discovery of the pregnancy dictates a marriage in time to legitimate the birth.

Such "shotgun" weddings are more likely to occur among white teenagers and among those from higher socioeconomic backgrounds (Furstenberg, 1976; Zelnik et al., 1981). However, even among these groups the number of such marriages is declining as out-of-wedlock childbirth becomes more accepted (Hartley, 1975).

Whether a teenager marries to legitimate her pregnancy or not, there are likely to be repercussions on her future marital experiences. Teenage marriages are at high risk for dissolution. Indeed, a number of studies have found that the age of the partners at marriage is positively related to long-range marital stability (e.g., Bumpass & Sweet, 1972; Card, 1977; Moore & Hofferth, 1977). A marriage that is compelled by accidental pregnancy may be even further at risk, since the partners may not want to be married to each other or, indeed, married at all. Moreover, marriages between individuals with limited education are at high risk for dissolution (Moore & Hofferth, 1977). When teenagers marry to legitimate a pregnancy, one or both often drop out of school to fulfill their new adult roles, thus incurring added risk to their marriage.

The high rate of dissolution of teenage marriages has important implications for adolescent mothers. Divorce has been identified as a major source of psychological stress and, for women especially, a common antecedent of psychological depression (Bloom, Asher, & White, 1978; Brown & Harris, 1978). Moreover, divorce also has negative economic consequences for women.

Even when such marriages remain intact, they may provide little economic stability. Card (1977) showed that the husbands of teenage mothers had lower educational attainment and jobs of lower occupational prestige than the husbands of a matched group of women who did not have children as teenagers. This was true whether or not the man was the father of the baby. Marecek (1979) reported similar findings. Thus the adolescent mother who marries is likely to have a husband with only limited earning power.

Subsequent Childbearing

Young women who bear their first child during adolescence are likely to get pregnant again sooner than women who bear their first child when they are in their twenties. For example, in one study of inner-city women, 47% of adolescents who gave birth were pregnant again within a year. Among older women, the rate of repeat pregnancy within a year was only 23% (Hardy, Welcher, Stanley, & Dallas, 1978). Not surprisingly, the completed family sizes of women who begin childbearing during adolescence are larger than those of women who begin later (Furstenberg, 1976). A number of reasons have been advanced for this high rate of repeat pregnancies. One possible explanation is simply that both the first pregnancy and those that follow result from an inability to use birth control reliably. If this were true, we might expect that teenagers would have high rates of repeat pregnancies even if the first pregnancy was terminated by an abortion. An alternative explanation, however, is that a birth signifies a transition to the role of mother, and continued childbearing may be in keeping with that role. Moreover, as Presser (1975) argued, the jobs open to teenage mothers may be so unattractive that full-time motherhood is more desirable. Thus it may be that having a child—not merely having been pregnant—determines the likelihood of further conceptions.

Whatever their causes, repeat births among teenagers have strong negative effects on young women's life chances. They may preclude further education and vocational preparation, thus preventing them from becoming economically self-sufficient. Moreover, a large number of children may drain the family's financial resources and be physically and emotionally debilitating.

CONSEQUENCES TO FAMILY MEMBERS

Thus far I have focused on the consequences of adolescent childbearing for the young mother. But there are consequences to others as well. In particular, the adolescent's family of origin may be deeply affected. Most who do not marry remain in their families of origin for at least some time after the baby is born. Researchers and service providers have found that the support of the girl's family—and especially of her mother—is critical in mitigating the effects of an early birth. What costs do a teenage mother's parents incur when they assume these responsibilities? In his study of inner-city adolescents who had given birth, Furstenberg (1980) found that most of them received both financial support and child care from their parents. Supporting an extra member may put a strain on the family's financial resources. Moreover, providing child care for the baby may cut into leisure time or work time. In some cases the baby's grandmother may have to quit work or postpone reentry into the work force so that she can take care of her grandchild while her daughter goes to school.

A baby may have both positive and negative effects on family harmony and the relationships among family members. One beneficial effect is that sharing the infant's care may produce greater closeness between parents and daughter. For example, about a third of the teenagers in Furstenberg's study reported that their relationships with their parents had improved in the year after the child was born (Furstenberg, 1980). But the greater attention paid to the young mother and her baby may have disadvantages for other siblings, who may find themselves unable to command as much of their parents' time.

Clinical studies carried out by family therapists at the Philadelphia Child Guidance Clinic have outlined some of the socioemotional tasks that must be accomplished when a teenager and her baby live with her family of origin (cited by Furstenberg, 1980). These include the ongoing negotiation of responsibility and authority for the baby as the young mother's child-care skills increase and as the child's needs change in the course of development. Also, accommodations must be made to the altered status of the young mother. Regardless of her chronological age, being a mother confers some degree of adult status on her. Nonetheless, in some situations it will be more appropriate to accord her the status congruent with her age rather than with her motherhood.

One of the benefits of adolescent childbearing is the pleasure the infant brings to the family. At least for inner-city teenagers, parental reactions to an out-of-wedlock pregnancy may be accepting or even positive (Flaherty et al., 1982; Furstenberg, 1980). Flaherty et al. found that, according to the teenagers, many parents took pleasure in the prospect of becoming grandparents. Unfortunately, such a positive response may encourage other children to follow their sister's example (Furstenberg, 1980).

At present most of our knowledge of how a girl's family of origin responds to an early birth is based on only a few studies, some of which were designed for other purposes. It should be noted that the response to a newborn may be quite different from the response to an older child. Also, the positive attention to a new mother and her baby may fade when the newness wears off. Moreover, if a teenager bears more than one child out of wedlock, the reception of the later births may be considerably cooler than that accorded the first one.

CONSEQUENCES TO ADOLESCENT FATHERS

Just as studies of the families of teenage mothers are few, so has little attention been paid to teenage fathers. Card's (1977) analysis of the PROJECT TALENT data is one of the few sources of such information. She found that boys who fathered a child during adolescence were more likely to drop out of school than members of a matched comparison group. At long-term follow-up, the former also held jobs with less prestige.

Being a father may also subject a young man to considerable emotional stress. Hendricks (1980) surveyed black teenagers from low-income backgrounds about their experiences as unwed fathers. He noted that many of these young men wanted to be actively involved with their children but were prevented by the young mother or her family. It was especially difficult to maintain a relationship with the child after the couple's relationship had ended. Another source of frustration was young fathers' inability to provide financial support for their children. Moreover, as Hendricks noted, unwed adolescent fathers suffer from the highly negative stereotypes that society at large holds of them.

Though the larger society may disapprove, fatherhood may be a social asset for young men from the inner city. Fathering a child can confer adult status; parenthood may signify maturity (cf. Phipps-

Yonas, 1980). Given the scarcity of employment in the inner city, becoming a father may be one of the few available means of acquiring adult status.

CONSEQUENCES TO THE CHILD

The developmental deficits for which children born to adolescent mothers are at risk have been well documented (e.g., Menken, 1972). For example, adolescents have higher rates of pregnancy complications such as toxemia and prolonged labor. Their infants have a higher incidence of low birthweight, cerebral palsy, epilepsy, and mental retardation. Some of these complications of pregnancy and delivery may be due to the mother's physical immaturity; however, inadequate prenatal nutrition and medical care are also important (Baldwin, 1976). Thus, serious as these physical problems are, their incidence could be reduced by improved medical care.

Intellectual Development

Leaving aside their elevated risk of mental retardation, the children of teenage mothers do not appear to have impaired cognitive abilities. Studies of the intelligence test scores of young children show little effect of the age of the mother (Cohen, Belmont, Dryfoos, Stein, & Zayac, 1980; Marecek, 1979). Nonetheless, Marecek found that such children were nearly three times as likely as children of older mothers to have failed first grade. Moreover, Card (1978) noted that when they reached adolescence children born to teenage mothers had lower academic abilities than children of older mothers.

Psychological Adjustment

Many concerns have been raised about the adequacy of young mothers' parenting and its effects on their children's psychosocial adjustment. The research in this area is at a rudimentary stage, and the findings are mixed. One of the earliest reports (DeLissovoy, 1973) claimed that adolescent parents rarely displayed warmth toward their children, used physical punishment frequently, and were intolerant of misbehavior. Marecek (1979) analyzed pediatricians' ratings of mothers' behavior during physical examinations of their infants at 4 months and 8 months of age. Relative to a comparison group of older black mothers, more black teenage mothers were rated as "unaware, unresponsive or slow in responding" to their children's needs and as having children who appeared "poorly cared for" at both examinations. In addition, at the 4-month examination teenage mothers were more likely to be rated as "underinvolved" in and "indifferent to" the examination proceedings; at the 8-month exam, more were rated as "rough" in their handling of their infants. Two additional studies based on observations of mothers with their infants (McLaughlin, Sandler, Sherrod, Vietze, & O'Connor, 1978; Osofsky & Osofsky, 1970) reported that, compared with older mothers, teenage mothers rated low on verbal interaction with their infants.

A much more positive view of teenage parenting is presented in studies by Furstenberg (1976) and Grow (1979). Furstenberg reported that only about 15% of the inner-city teenagers he studied could be described as rejecting or problem-prone mothers; the others were reported to be deeply involved with their children. Similarly, relying on mothers' responses to interviews and questionnaires, Grow concluded that most of a sample of urban white teenagers found motherhood demanding but highly satisfying. Moreover, most were judged to be effective parents.

These disparate findings cannot be easily synthesized. The studies involve diverse methods and target a range of maternal behaviors. Moreover, the samples involve mothers from different backgrounds and children at different stages of development. Thus it would be premature to try to identify consistent themes or styles that characterize the maternal behavior of adolescent childbearers. But it does appear that when direct observation rather than maternal self-report is used, inadequacies in teenagers' parenting skills are in evidence. These inadequacies may affect their children's psychological and behavioral adjustment.

Another issue that is frequently raised is whether adolescents are more likely to physically abuse or neglect their children than older mothers. For example, Bolton (1980) speculated that teenage mothers are at high risk for child abuse, based on the high degree of similarity between the statistical profiles of adolescent childbearers and child abusers. Similarly, Nortman (1974) found higher mortality rates among preschool children of teenage mothers; she attributed them to household accidents stemming from parental neglect. Nonetheless, there is no direct evidence that, net of other factors, bearing children as a teenager raises a woman's risk of abusing or neglecting them (Kinard & Klerman, 1980).

Studies of the psychosocial adjustment and behavioral characteristics of children born to adolescents are sparse and contradictory. Osofsky and Osofsky (1970) reported that such infants were rated normal in level of physical activity but low in responsiveness and affect. In a study of pediatricians' ratings of infants' behavior at 8 months of age, Marecek (1983) found that the infants of black teenagers were more likely than the infants of older mothers to be rated "passive" in responding to physical stimuli and "overly apprehensive" of the pediatrician.

Furstenberg (1976) used a doll-play technique to study the psychosocial adjustment of the children of black teenagers from the inner city. He rated children who were between 3.5 and 5 years of age on indexes of deferral of gratification, efficacy, trust, and self-esteem. Age of the mother per se did not affect ratings on these indexes. But circumstances such as economic deprivation and lack of contact with a father figure did affect adjustment, and these circumstances were more likely to be present in the lives of children born to adolescents.

Using ratings made by psychological testers and data from maternal interviews, Marecek (1983) studied the psychosocial adjustment of children born to a group of inner-city black teenagers. Based on data collected at 4 and 7 years of age, it appeared that they were likely to lag in the development of self-control, as evidenced by lack of persistence in working toward a goal, low frustration tolerance, and undercontrol of behavior. For boys, lack of control over aggression was also more frequent; it was manifested in resistiveness and hostility toward the psychological tester and maternal reports of fighting with peers and of taking peers' toys. Girls were reported to experience a greater incidence of phobias and excessive bed-wetting.

These studies of the psychosocial and behavioral characteristics of children born to adolescents do not provide enough information to give a systematic account of teenagers' maternal behavior or of their offspring's psychosocial development. Nonetheless, the results obtained thus far suggest that such children run an elevated risk of psychosocial problems, even though many of them make adequate adjustments.

CONSEQUENCES TO SOCIETY

The social costs of having large numbers of adolescents give birth are heavy. Many teenagers will require financial assistance from public sources in order to support their children. Moreover, early childbearing is associated with larger family sizes, thus increasing family financial needs. In addition, adolescents' higher risk of prenatal and perinatal complications translates into higher medical costs for themselves and for their children. These medical costs are often borne by society, as are the costs of any social services that an adolescent mother or her children may require.

Adolescent childbearing may entail social costs beyond the monetary ones. Most adolescent births result from unplanned pregnancies. Thus many young women and at least some young men may enter adulthood with their aspirations thwarted by premature and unwanted parenthood. Moreover, the large number of adolescent births out of wedlock may have negative social repercussions. As Zelnik et al. (1981) remind us, a child's status as "legitimate" serves to allocate responsibility for his or her care and placement in society. Illegitimacy on a large scale threatens the integrity and continuity of society by undermining the mechanisms for socializing new generations. Finally, the larger family sizes of adolescent childbearers may have negative social implications. Though large families are idealized in our culture, there are few societal benefits of increased population size, either nationally or worldwide.

THE CONSEQUENCES OF INDUCED ABORTION

CONSEQUENCES TO THE TEENAGER

Abortion seems to have fewer and less protracted socioeconomic consequences for a teenager than carrying a pregnancy to term and raising the child. From the standpoint of individual expense, the economic costs of abortion are modest. Although having an abortion requires that a young woman raise a sum of money on short notice, once the abortion is performed there are no financial obligations in the future.

The interpersonal consequences of an abortion center mainly on the possible damage to a young woman's relationships if her abortion is against others' wishes or moral standards. For example, having an abortion against her parents' wishes may injure her relationship with them. If the father of the baby is opposed, it might jeopardize her relationship to him. Moreover, an abortion may damage a young woman's standing among her peers. A study of inner-city teenagers showed that most opposed abortion on moral or ethical grounds. Common sentiments were that abortion is the equivalent of murder and that it is an evasion of the just punishment for having sex (Flaherty et al., 1982). Thus ostracism or moral condemnation by one's peer group is a possible negative outcome of an abortion.

At present, a teenager in some jurisdictions has control over the interpersonal consequences of having an abortion because she decides who shall be privy to the information that she is seeking or has had an abortion (see Melton & Pliner, this volume). Except insofar as she must confide in others to obtain their assistance in making the practical arrangements, a teenager in such states can keep her abortion entirely secret. But if statutes are passed that require parental notification or consent as a condition for adolescent abortion, her privacy would be seriously limited.

Psychological Effects of Abortion

One of the myths about abortion is that women feel deep regret and self-reproach afterward. The experience is expected to generate long-standing emotional damage. Studies of women's attitudes and psychological well-being following abortion do not support these contentions (see generally Adler & Dolcini, this volume). For example, Ekblad (1955) found that only 14% of Swedish women who had abortions experienced regrets and that all of the few women who had serious emotional difficulties after abortion had previous histories of emotional disorder. A later study by Kummer (1963) surveyed 32 psychiatrists about their clinical experiences with women who had had abortions. All the psychiatrists agreed that severe emotional consequences never or seldom occurred. Indeed, the predominant emotion that women report after abortion is a sense of relief. It should be noted that these studies did not focus specifically on adolescents. Nonetheless, in the absence of data to the contrary, there is no reason to assume that adolescents' responses to abortion would reflect more emotional distress than those of adult women. As Adler and Dolcini (this volume) show, whatever age differences there are tend to be small and to reflect age differences in the social circumstances in which pregnant females find themselves. Severe emotional responses are very rare.

In addition to disputing the negative psychological consequences, the empirical research offers some evidence that there may be positive changes in personality consequent to abortion. For example, contraceptive use tends to improve (cf. Nadelson, 1978). Freeman (1977) suggested that this is due not simply to the "scare" the woman has had but to a deeper personality change. She found that after an abortion women reported feeling more instrumental and self-directed. While this finding needs to be replicated and extended to teenagers, it suggests that success in obtaining an abortion increases a woman's sense of autonomy and efficacy. Such a positive effect might be more pronounced among adolescents because they have so few experiences of autonomy and control in the course of their daily lives.

Consequences of Refused Abortion

In addition to the consequences of abortion, we must also consider the consequences of denying abortions to women who want them. Given Freeman's (1977) finding that obtaining an abortion increased feelings of self-directedness, being denied an abortion might well increase feelings of victimization and impotence.

A number of studies have documented negative effects of denied abortion on the subsequent mother/child relationship (e.g., Caplan, 1954). Moreover, others found serious impairments in children's mental and physical capacities and problems of adjustment (David & Matejcek, 1981; Hook, 1963). In a 21-year follow-up of children born after denial of an abortion, Forssman and Thuwe (1966) identified numerous areas in which the children in the sample were deficient relative to matched controls. Most of these studies were carried out on adult women living in Western European countries. We cannot know for sure that the experiences of American teenagers will parallel those of the women studied, but there is little reason to expect that outcomes for their offspring would be more positive. In any case, it is important to document the consequences of refusing abortion. Legislative restrictions on access may well prevent teenagers from obtaining abortions.

Societal Consequences of Abortion

It is difficult to document the societal consequences of abortion. Nonetheless, there has been considerable speculation about what these consequences are. One common contention is that access to abortion leads to casual use of contraception. There is at least circumstantial evidence that this contention is false. For example, the rate of pregnancies terminated by abortion has remained fairly stable for a number of years, which argues against the notion that there has been a wholesale abandonment of contraception in favor of abortion. Moreover, the finding that women become better contraceptive users after having abortions similarly suggests that access to abortion does not interfere with contraception.

It is also claimed that abortion shows lack of respect for life and that permitting abortions diminishes respect for life even further. The first contention rests on the idea that life begins at the moment of conception, a view that can be neither defended nor disputed by empirical evidence. Those who support free access to abortion hold a different view and thus cannot be accused of lacking respect for life.

Unlike the more conservative elements of society, many feminists view abortion as having positive societal consequences. They posit an essential relation between access to abortion and equality of rights for women. Control over one's body is seen as being a fundamental human right and as including control over one's reproductive capacity. Access to abortion is regarded as necessary to ensure women control over reproduction; thus it is seen as an essential aspect of social equality for women.

CONCLUSION

This review summarizes the social research on the consequences of adolescent childbearing and abortion. This research suggests that there are often negative repercussions when teenagers bear children, though there may be benefits as well. Abortion seems to lead to fewer negative outcomes. In making this assessment, I do not mean to imply that decisions about adolescent abortion can be made within a consequentialist framework. Rather, this review is offered as a means of grounding the discussion in the reality of teenagers' lives. The legal, ethical, and moral issues raised by adolescent abortion need to be debated on their own terms; the information here underscores the practical significance of such debates.

References

Baldwin, W. (1976). Adolescent pregnancy and childbearing—growing concerns for Americans. *Population Bulletin, 31*, 22–23.

Baldwin, W. (1978). Statement on adolescent childbearing in the United States—1976. Given before the Subcommittee on Select Education of the House of Representatives (July 24, 1978). Washington, DC: U.S. Government Printing Office.

Bloom, B. L., Asher, S. J., & White, S. W. (1978). Marital disruption as a stressor: A review and analysis. *Psychological Bulletin, 85*, 867–894.

Bolton, F. G. (1980). *The pregnant adolescent*. Beverly Hills, CA: Sage.

Brown, G. W., & Harris, T. (1978). *Social origins of depression: A study of psychiatric disorder in women*. New York: Free Press.

Bumpass, L., & Sweet, J. (1972). Differentials in marital instability: 1970. *American Sociological Review, 37*, 754–766.

Caplan, G. (1954). The disturbance of the mother-child relationship by unsuccessful attempts at abortion. *Mental Hygiene, 38*, 67–80.

Card, J. J. (1977). *Consequences of adolescent childbearing for the young parent's future personal and professional life*. Palo Alto, CA: American Institutes of Research.

Card, J. J. (1978). *Long-term consequences for children born to adolescent parents*. Palo Alto, CA: American Institutes of Research.

Cohen, P. J., Belmont, L., Dryfoos, J., Stein, Z., & Zayac, S. (1980). Maternal age and children's intelligence. *Social Biology, 27*, 138–154.

David, H. P., & Matejcek, Z. (1981). Children born to women denied abortion: An update. *Family Planning Perspectives, 13*, 32–34.

DeLissovoy, V. (1973). Child care by adolescent parents. *Children Today, 2*, 22–25.

Ekblad, N. (1955). Induced abortion on psychiatric grounds. *Acta Psychiatrica Scandinavica Supplementum, 99*.

Flaherty, E. W., Marecek, J., Olsen, K., & Wilcove, G. (1982). *Psychological factors associated with fertility regulation among adolescents*. Philadelphia: Philadelphia Health Management Corporation.

Forssman, H., & Thuwe, I. (1963). One hundred and twenty children born after application for therapeutic abortion refused: Their mental health, social adjustment and educational level up to the age of 21. *Acta Psychiatrica Scandinavica Supplementum, 168*.

Freeman, E. (1977). Influence of personality attributes on abortion experiences. *American Journal of Orthopsychiatry, 47*, 503–513.

Furstenberg, F. F. (1976). *Unplanned parenthood: The social consequences of teenage childbearing.* New York: Macmillan.

Furstenberg, F. F. (1980). Burdens and benefits: The impact of early childbearing on the family. *Journal of Social Issues, 36,* 64–87.

Grow, L. (1979). *Early childrearing by young mothers.* New York: Child Welfare League.

Hardy, J. B., Welcher, D. W., Stanley, J., & Dallas, J. R. (1978). The long-range outcome of adolescent pregnancy. *Clinical Obstetrics and Gynecology, 21,* 4.

Hartley, S. (1975). *Illegitimacy.* Berkeley, CA: University of California Press.

Hendricks, L. E. (1980). Unwed adolescent fathers: Problems they face and their sources of social support. *Adolescence, 15,* 861–869.

Hook, K. (1966). Refused abortion: A follow-up study of two hundred and forty-nine women whose applications were refused by the national board of health in Sweden. *Acta Psychiatrica Scandinavica, 42,* 71–88.

Kamerman, S. B. (1979). Work and family in industrialized societies. *Signs, 4,* 632–650.

Kinard, E. M., & Klerman, L. V. (1980). Teenage parenting and child abuse: Are they related? *American Journal of Orthopsychiatry, 50,* 481–487.

Kummer, J. (1963). Post abortion psychiatric illness—a myth? *American Journal of Psychiatry, 119,* 980–983.

Marecek, J. (1979). Economic, social, and psychological consequences of adolescent childbearing (Contract No. NO1-HD-7Z806). Bethesda, MD: National Institute of Child Health and Human Development.

Marecek, J. (1983). *The cognitive and psychosocial development of children born to inner-city adolescent mothers.* Unpublished manuscript, Swarthmore College, Swarthmore, PA.

McLaughlin, J., Sandler, H. M., Sherrod, K., Vietze, P. J. M., & O'Connor, S. (1978). *Social-psychological characteristics of adolescent mothers and behavioral characteristics of their first-born children.* Unpublished manuscript, Vanderbilt University, Nashville, TN.

McLaughlin, S. D. (1977). *Consequences of adolescent childbearing for the mother's occupational attainment.* Washington, DC: Urban Institute.

Menken, J. (1972). The health and social consequences of teenage childbearing. *Family Planning, 4,* 45–53.

Moore, K. J., & Hofferth, S. (1977). *The consequences of early childbearing:*

An analysis of selected parental outcomes using two longitudinal data sets. Washington, DC: Urban Institute.

Moore, K., & Waite, L. (1977). Early childbearing and educational attainment. *Family Planning Perspectives, 9,* 220–225.

Nadelson, C. C. (1978). The emotional impact of abortion. In M. Notman & C. C. Nadelson (Eds.), *The woman patient* (Vol. 1). New York: Plenum.

Nortman, D. (1974). Parental age as a factor in pregnancy outcome and child development. *Reports on Population/Family Planning, 16,* 1–51.

Osofsky, H., & Osofsky, J. (1970). The adolescent as mother: Factors related to their children's development. *American Journal of Orthopsychiatry, 40,* 328.

Phipps-Yonas, S. (1980). Teenage pregnancy and motherhood: A review of the literature. *American Journal of Orthopsychiatry, 50,* 403–431.

Presser, H. (1975). *Female employment and the first birth.* Paper presented at the American Sociological Association meetings.

Zelnik, M., Kantner, J. F., & Ford, K. (1981). *Sex and pregnancy in adolescence.* Beverly Hills, CA: Sage.

Zero Population Growth. (1977). *Teenage pregnancy: A major problem for minors.* Washington, DC: Author.

ELIZABETH S. SCOTT

Legal and Ethical Issues in Counseling Pregnant Adolescents

Mental health professionals who work with adolescents may on occasion deal with clients who are making difficult decisions relating to pregnancy and abortion. Although the problem of teenage pregnancy is certainly not new, the availability of abortion in recent years creates unique clinical and ethical issues for the mental health professional. In *City of Akron v. Akron Center for Reproductive Health*,[1] the United States Supreme Court adopted the position argued by the American Psychological Association[2] and struck down the Akron ordinance requiring that abortion counseling be done by a physician. This holding, in effect, invited psychologists and other mental health professionals to assume a larger role in counseling pregnant teenagers and providing information relevant to abortion. Aside from abortion counselors, however, mental health professionals in many settings—schools, outpatient mental health clinics, and other health care facilities—are counseling pregnant teens and adopting a role that presents new challenges, both in the exercise of clinical skills and in the complexity of the ethical and legal considerations involved (Scott, 1984).

The adolescent client grappling with the decision of whether to have an abortion or continue the pregnancy faces a crisis that is

1. 103 S.Ct. 2481 (1983).
2. *Id.*, brief of amicus curiae Am. Psychological Ass'n.

frightening to many mature adult women. This critical decision is made under conditions that inevitably involve time pressure. Some girls may have no adult support other than the therapist; indeed, the counselor may be the only adult who is aware of the pregnancy (Torres, Forrest, & Eisman, 1980). Other teenagers may experience considerable pressure from parents or others to make a particular decision (Chesler & Davis, 1980). Many may turn to the therapist to provide guidance and even to relieve them of responsibility for the decision.

The situation of the teenager contemplating abortion and the role of the therapist are complicated by the ethical and legal dimensions of teenage abortion (Scott, 1984). Questions may arise in the counseling relationship about whether the girl should consult her parents, whether she has the maturity to make the decision independently, and whether the counseling relationship and the abortion itself may be conducted privately. These issues and the more general one of the appropriate role of the counselor may all involve legal as well as ethical and clinical concerns. The law regarding adolescent abortion is in some states complex and ambiguous (Melton, 1983). Nonetheless, the legal, ethical, and psychological dimensions of the abortion decision are so interwoven that the clinician who hopes to provide effective assistance requires an understanding of the legal context. The teenager must understand how to proceed if she chooses abortion and must know the requirements imposed by the law; the counselor may assist her in these efforts.

Important ethical dimensions of the clinician's role may also be affected by the legal framework. Concerns of professional ethics such as the protection of confidentiality, respect for client autonomy and privacy, and the responsibility to act in the client's interest (American Psychological Association, 1981) may be either undermined or supported by the law in a given state. An ethical issue that is unique to this context is the role of the clinician's own views on abortion and the effect they may have on the counseling relationship. In general, the ethical contours of this professional role are complex and merit careful examination.

Under some state laws, mental health professionals may be called upon to participate in the abortion decision by rendering an opinion on the maturity of an individual adolescent seeking abortion or on whether the abortion is in the girl's best interest (Melton, 1983; Scott, 1984). The clinician's opinion may carry great weight; indeed, it may be the decisive factor in many cases. This non-therapeutic role raises many concerns for clinicians, especially when the therapist has previously had a treatment relationship with the individual.

This chapter will examine many of the issues that concern mental health professionals counseling adolescents who are contemplating abortion. I will examine the relevance of the legal framework to the counseling role and also explore the therapist's role in assisting the teenager to make an informed, thoughtful decision. Involvement of the parents in the abortion decision will be addressed from clinical, ethical, and legal perspectives, and I will explore issues relating to confidentiality and legal regulation and limitation of the adolescent's privacy. Finally, I will look at the legal and ethical issues raised when the clinician assumes an evaluative role in the abortion decision.

THE LEGAL FRAMEWORK: THE SUPREME COURT'S UNCLEAR GUIDANCE

There is a substantial body of constitutional law dealing with the adolescent's right to make a private independent abortion decision and the extent to which that right may be limited by the parents or the state (Bush, 1982; Garvey, 1978). Teenage abortion is also subject to statutory regulation in most states (Scott, 1984). This in itself makes abortion more complex than many other issues that may arise in therapy. The situation is further complicated because the nature of the minor's constitutional abortion rights remains somewhat unclear and because legal regulation varies from state to state.

The Supreme Court, in its several pronouncements regarding adolescent abortion since *Danforth v. Planned Parenthood of Central*

Missouri[3] in 1976, has given somewhat uncertain guidance (see Melton & Pliner, this volume). Since the Supreme Court's 1983 decision, *City of Akron,* some things are clear; a minor is constitutionally entitled to obtain an abortion without the involvement of her parents if she can establish, through some clearly defined and confidential procedure, that she has the maturity to make the decision. The Supreme Court held in *H. L. v. Matheson*[4] that the Utah statute requiring notice to parents of their child's abortion decision is constitutionally acceptable for immature minors. The Court implied in *Matheson* (and supported in dicta in *Akron*), but has not held, that such a requirement may not be acceptable for mature minors.[5] Further, the plurality opinion in *Bellotti v. Baird*[6] indicated that the immature minor may have a right to show that abortion is in her best interest.

The response of states to the Supreme Court's guidelines has varied (Bush, 1983). Some states do not distinguish minors from adults for the purpose of consenting to abortion. Both are presumed to be competent to make the decision; the teenager is merely subject to the generally applicable requirements to provide informed consent. Wyoming, for example, defines "woman" in its abortion statute as "any female person, whether an adult or minor."[7] Other states have restricted minors' rights to the extent that the Court has allowed. Some have adopted the *Bellotti* guidelines requiring the minor to establish in a judicial proceeding that she is mature enough to make her own decision or that it is in her best interest to obtain an abortion.[8] Others have notice requirements like the Utah statute approved in *Matheson.*[9]

3. 428 U.S. 52 (1976).

4. 450 U.S. 398 (1981).

5. The Court noted that the minor petitioners in *Matheson* made no claim that they were mature minors. In *Akron,* the Court asserted in a footnote that notice to parents of mature minors would be unconstitutional. 10 S.Ct. at 2499 n.31. However, the ordinance in question did not have a notice requirement. Therefore the statement is dicta (i.e., not the holding and, therefore, not binding precedent).

6. 443 U.S. 622 (1979).

7. WYO. STAT. § 35-6-10(a)(viii) (1977).

8. MINN. STAT. § 525-56 (Cum. Supp. 1982).

9. MD. ANN. CODE art. 43 § 135(1) (1980).

At least in some states it is clear that the legal course open to minors contemplating abortion may appear rather difficult. The Supreme Court describes the hearing to prove maturity as an avenue to abortion for the girl reluctant to consult her parents, but it may seem like a frightening path to a pregnant adolescent who is likely to lack familiarity with the legal process. Although in one state an adolescent may be able to simply go to a clinic and request an abortion, in another she may be required to petition a court and go through a hearing. Practice may even vary among states with similar laws or within states. In one jurisdiction the minor's competence to give informed consent may be informally assessed by an abortion counselor or physician. In another, the minor who seeks abortion may need an attorney to help her deal with the rigorous scrutiny of her maturity that will be required.

Clinicians working with teenagers making abortion decisions may better assist their clients if they are familiar not only with their general constitutional and legal rights but also with the process by which legal regulation in their state is implemented. The clinician's familiarity with local judicial practice and appropriate referral sources for legal counsel may be very important to adolescent clients in jurisdictions that create barriers to their access to abortion. Abortion counselors, of course, will view providing this kind of information as part of their role; other mental health professionals who encounter pregnant teens in their clinical work may also serve their clients better if they are knowledgable about legal requirements and restrictions.

THE CLINICIAN AS COUNSELOR

The clinician, whether abortion counselor or therapist, typically has two roles in assisting the pregnant adolescent girl. The first is to assist her in examining all alternatives, thus increasing the likelihood that her ultimate decision is mature, independent, and carefully deliberated (Brown, 1983). The second role is to provide support through the decision-making process and through the abortion or pregnancy itself (Chesler & Davis, 1980; Dornblaser, 1981).

For the pregnant teenager, making an informed decision involves weighing the alternatives available to her. The counselor may wish to explore with her the implications of continuing with the pregnancy and putting the child up for adoption, of marrying the father and keeping the baby, of continuing to live at home with the baby, and of abortion (American Academy of Pediatrics, 1979). The implications each of these alternatives may have for the girl's future may merit careful investigation.

There are several possibilities available if the pregnancy is continued. The counselor may wish to have some general familiarity with adoption procedures if the client is considering this alternative. If the adolescent anticipates keeping the child, the therapist may wish to explore with her the effect that this decision will have on her future educational and employment opportunities (Card & Wise, 1978; Trussell, 1976). The girl should know that under federal laws pregnant teenagers and teenage parents can no longer be excluded from public schools. She should also be aware of the possibility of public assistance and child-care facilities. However, the clinician may also feel a responsibility to emphasize the difficulties of raising a child as a teenage parent, either married or single (Furstenburg, 1976a; Marecek, this volume). Social science research suggests that teenage mothers often do not complete their high-school education. Only 18% of young women who bear children when they are under 18 finish high school, compared with 55% of those who postpone childbirth until after age 18 (Trussell, 1976). It may be important to the minor to realize that many teenagers are unable to handle the substantial difficulties of caring for a child and going to school despite the absence of legal barriers. Employment opportunities are also less available to teenage mothers, who are concentrated in lower-paying unskilled jobs (Card & Wise, 1978).

The teenager who is exploring the idea of marriage should understand the stresses associated with that decision. Of those adolescent girls who continue with the pregnancy, almost half eventually marry the father of the child (Furstenburg, 1976a). Not surprisingly, a very high percentage of these marriages end in divorce; one study indicated that 60% of teenage marriages involving a premarital pregnancy ended within six years (Furstenburg, 1976b).

The empirical trends regarding marriage, education, and employment (see Marecek, this volume) are not predictive of the future in any individual case. However, it is important that the adolescent deciding between abortion and other alternatives understand the problems associated with each course.

In terms of abortion itself, the adolescent considering that alternative may be greatly assisted by information about legal regulations, procedures, and local practice. Several things may be relevant here. If the state law requires that notice of the abortion be given to parents, this will be important information for the adolescent. The Supreme Court seemed to suggest in *Matheson* and *Akron* that the notice requirements may be constitutionally invalid as applied to mature minors. However, most notice statutes do not include this exception or allow the minor an avenue to prove her maturity and thereby prevent notification to her parents of the abortion (Bush, 1983). This ambiguity may create an uncomfortable dilemma for clinicians and counselors advising their teenage clients concerning the implications of their abortion decision. If state practice includes routine notice to parents without an inquiry into the minor's maturity, an agency may seek an attorney general's opinion to establish a policy that protects the constitutional rights of mature minors. In individual cases, referral to legal counsel may be indicated.

Several states have adopted the procedure approved by the court in *Bellotti v. Baird* and require a judicial hearing to determine whether the minor seeking abortion is mature or, alternatively, whether the abortion is in her best interest (Bush, 1983). In these states the clinician may describe to the minor the steps needed to meet the legal requirements and may also provide information about legal counsel. In Massachusetts, the Woman's Bar Association provides free legal counsel in adolescent abortion cases. Further, abortions under the Massachusetts post-*Bellotti* statute are routinely approved by judges (Mnookin, 1983). This type of information may be very helpful to the teenager. The abortion counselor, of course, will have information about both the legal requirements and the local practice and procedure. The clinician who is not an abortion counselor may find it useful to seek information from the Planned Parenthood Association or to refer the teenager to this agency for assistance.

For the girl who resolves to have an abortion after carefully considering the alternatives, the counseling process promotes the legal objective that the medical decision be an informed one. Although the counseling may have a broader scope than the requirements of the law for informed consent to the medical decision, the girl who has worked through the decision to abort may be more likely to meet the legal requirements (Lidz et al., 1984).

VOLUNTARINESS OF THE ABORTION DECISION

The legal determination of whether valid informed consent to abortion has been obtained should include a finding that the decision is voluntary (Meisel, 1979; Weithorn & Campbell, 1982). This is also of concern to the clinician working with the pregnant adolescent. The primary goal of the abortion counselor is to help the teenager to carefully weigh her choices and reach the decision she accepts as best for her (American Academy of Pediatrics, 1979). This objective is consistent with the legal requirement that the individual giving consent not be coerced and not passively accept a decision made by someone else (Nadelson, 1974). This may be a difficult goal to realize, since teenagers frequently are subject to substantial pressure in this situation. Parents who are aware of their daughter's pregnancy may have strong views about the appropriate course (Chesler & Davis, 1980).

Although the law has focused on the issue of the minor's right to seek an abortion without parental involvement (Melton, 1983), much of the clinical literature on abortion counseling suggests that frequently the *parents* want the abortion and the minor resists

(Nadelson, 1974). Although the Supreme Court has never addressed the issue, lower courts have held that a minor may not be required to have an abortion against her will.[10] Of course this does not resolve the issue of parental pressure either for or against abortion. The clinician in this situation may perform a valuable role by clarifying the importance, from both a legal and a psychological perspective, of the girl's right to make an independent decision for which she assumes responsibility.

Another source of coercion may be the father of the child, who may have a strong preference for abortion or for keeping the child. Where the father wants the girl to continue the pregnancy, there is an ethical issue of his right as the infant's father to have a role in the decision. The Supreme Court has made it clear, however, that since the mother is most involved and burdened by the pregnancy and the birth of the child, the father has no legal right to veto an abortion decision or even to receive notice of the mother's choice.[11]

The clinician's role in protecting the pregnant adolescent against coercion as she struggles with this decision may be delicate and difficult. The girl may wish to abdicate responsibility and allow others to make the decision. Even if she has a strong preference, she may be reluctant to resist pressure from her parents or boyfriend. Helping the girl accept responsibility for this decision is an important clinical objective that helps meet the legal requirement of voluntariness (Joffe, 1978). This is not to say that the decision being urged upon the girl is erroneous simply because parents or boyfriend or friends are exerting pressure. The clinical and legal objective is that she consider all the alternatives and reach her own decision.

THE ROLE OF PARENTS

The clinician working with the pregnant adolescent may conclude that it is clinically desirable that the girl's parents be aware of the

10. *In re* Smith, 16 Md. App. 209, 295 A.2d 238 (1972).
11. Planned Parenthood of Cent. Mo. v. Danforth, 428 U.S. 52 (1976).

pregnancy so they can support her during the stressful decision period (American Academy of Pediatrics, 1979; Brown, 1983; Gedan, 1974). Absent unusual circumstances, the teenager in any crisis situation may benefit from the support of parents, and it may be sound clinical practice to encourage their involvement. There is empirical evidence that it is beneficial to teenagers undergoing abortion to have such support (Bracken, Hachamovitch, & Grossman, 1974). One study also indicated that pregnant teenagers overestimated the negativity of their parents' reactions (Furstenburg, 1976a). Thus an important issue in the relationship between the therapist and the adolescent client may be whether the parents should be consulted about the pregnancy.

This issue of whether the parents' participation in therapy may be valuable to the adolescent dealing with particular problems may arise in many clinical settings. Where the "problem" is pregnancy, however, the issue arises in a legal setting that may be relevant to the clinical decision making. If notice to parents of the abortion is required, this may promote their involvement in the counseling. Helping the teenager deal with her parents' knowledge about her pregnancy and abortion will be an important clinical issue. If the therapist believes that notice to her parents would be truly detrimental to her, a more difficult situation exists. If the clinician is persuaded that harm may come to the pregnant teenager if her parents are notified of the abortion, she may be referred to legal counsel. Notice to parents may not be required where serious harm is likely to result.[12]

Other problems may arise in states where the minor has the right to obtain an abortion privately without notice to her parents. The counselor who believes that a particular pregnant teenager needs the support of her parents during this difficult period may face an ethical dilemma. Attempting to persuade her to tell her parents about the abortion may be encouraging her to give up a legal right. Some clinicians may feel it is appropriate to freely explore with the teenager the benefits and problems of informing

12. H. L. v. Matheson, 480 U.S. 398 (1981).

her parents and that the clinician's own views may be expressed as long as the adolescent's right to have a private abortion is emphasized. The therapist who feels strongly that the girl's parents should be involved in the decision making may wish to refer the case to another clinician.

The mental health professional faces particularly complex ethical issues when the parents request therapy for their daughter. It will be very important at the outset to explore the girl's preferences about counseling and to determine whether the treatment is in her best interests (Division of Child, Youth, and Family Services, 1982). Some parents may seek to enlist the clinician in persuading the girl to make a particular decision about the pregnancy. The therapist is ethically bound to clarify the nature of the professional relationships with both the parents and the child in this situation (APA, 1981). This clarification will include the extent of the parents' participation in the counseling and any limitations on confidentiality between the counselor and the adolescent client.

CONFIDENTIALITY OF THE COUNSELOR/CLIENT RELATIONSHIP

Related to the issue of parental involvement in the abortion decision is the extent to which the confidentiality of the relationship between the clinician and the adolescent client is legally protected. State laws vary regarding protection of confidentiality in psychotherapy and counseling involving minors. In some states minors have a right to seek outpatient mental health treatment without their parents' consent (Wadlington, 1983). Thus the therapy relationship is protected even if under other statutory provisions notice to parents of abortion may be required. Alternatively, a state may recognize the minor's right to a private abortion but have no statutory provision that the minor may consent to mental health treatment independently. In this situation there may be a question whether the abortion counseling is protected from disclosure even though the abortion itself may be confidential.

It is clear that state laws do not always reflect a consistent and uniform policy toward the minor's right of privacy. The law may reflect inconsistencies between the constitutional protection of the adolescent's autonomy and privacy in the abortion context and the general legal presumption on other issues that parents have a right to be involved in, and in fact to make decisions affecting, their child's welfare. For example, a school counselor wishing to refer a pregnant teenager to a family planning clinic may be faced with a legal requirement that all referrals to physicians or mental health professionals be done with parental consent. The counselor in this situation may refer the issue to the school system's attorney; an attorney general's opinion may clarify the superior status of the minor's constitutional right of privacy and interpret the education regulations in a way consistent with this right.

Another problem may arise where parents have a right of access to their minor children's medical and mental health records under Buckley-type amendments to the state's Freedom of Information Act. In some states, such as Virginia, even though minors may obtain an abortion without significant barriers, it is not clear that parents' right of access to their medical records is suspended.[13] The application of such laws to abortion records seems to be unconstitutional; however, until they are challenged, they continue to create an ambiguous legal situation. Again, an attorney general's opinion may clarify ambiguity and set policy. However, this may not help the clinician and the adolescent client dealing with an immediate problem.

Psychologists and other therapists are bound by an obligation to preserve confidentiality with their clients to the extent possible; that obligation applies to therapeutic relationships with minors as well. A recent proposed revision of the Ethical Principles of Psychologists (APA, 1981) recommends that in working with minors and families, psychologists be sensitive to each individual's right of confidentiality while also considering where the intrafamilial sharing of clinicial or evaluative information is in the client's best interest (Division of Child, Youth, and Family Services, 1982). In

13. VA. CODE ANN. § 21-342(b)(3) (1968).

counseling a teenager who is deciding about an abortion, it is particularly important that the mental health professional be familiar with any legal limitations on confidentiality. The clinician will want to describe clearly the parameters of the confidential relationship and the circumstances in which disclosure to parents or others may be required.

THE CLINICIAN'S PERSONAL VALUES AND THE COUNSELING RELATIONSHIP

Abortion is an issue that evokes strong moral and emotional responses in many people; teenage abortion is even more controversial. Some clinicians may be personally opposed to abortion. Others may believe it is never desirable for an adolescent to have a baby because of the enormous potential costs to her future development. Strong personal beliefs may create an ethical dilemma for the clinician attempting to help the adolescent make a decision that represents the client's best interests (Brown, 1983; Joffe, 1978).

Abortion counselors are unlikely to be generally opposed to abortion on ethical grounds. Other clinicians, however, may well have strong negative views, based on religious or ethical concerns, and may find objectivity in counseling the adolescent considering this course very difficult. A counselor who believes that abortion is morally wrong should think about referring the pregnant teenager to another clinician (American Academy of Pediatrics, 1979). Serious problems of professional ethics arise if the clinician's personal values interfere with the ability to assist clients in weighing the alternatives (Joffe, 1978). Principle 3c of the Ethical Principles of Psychologists (APA, 1981) directs that actions be avoided that would diminish clients' legal rights. Abortion, for the mature minor, is a legal right that has been designated as having constitutional status. Psychologists whose values lead them, either consciously or unconsciously, to discourage consideration of abortion may violate professional ethics.

The ethical issue for the professional abortion counselor may also be acute. Abortion counseling as a profession grew out of an advocacy movement that aimed to make abortion widely available and to promote favorable laws (Joffe, 1978). Many abortion counselors may have a bias in favor of abortion and believe that other alternatives are generally inappropriate for adolescents. Indeed, for the clinician who does not morally oppose abortion there may be a presumptive preference for this alternative. Concerned with the impact of pregnancy and childbirth on a young girl's life and aware of the empirical research on the dismal educational and employment prospects of the unwed mother, a counselor may find it hard to maintain neutrality when helping a confused and ambivalent teenager make the choice between abortion or continuing with the pregnancy. The abortion counseling literature emphasizes the importance of maintaining neutrality and helping the girl consider all the alternatives available to her (Brown, 1983; Marcus, 1979; Nadelson, 1974). In some cases the temptation to encourage abortion may be great.

The extent to which a therapist or an abortion counselor should counsel in favor of or against abortion is an ethical issue that must be resolved by the individual clinician. The counselor who has personal views on abortion is not necessarily disabled from helping the teenager decide what is best for her. However, it may be important for the therapist to examine the extent to which a strong personal perspective may affect clinicial judgment. It may be appropriate to openly acknowledge personal values to the client, offering the option of referral to another therapist.

Deciding whether to obtain an abortion may be very stressful for adolescents. Particularly younger teens may be more easily influenced in their choice than adults because they generally have less experience with autonomy and independent decision making. Thus they may rely heavily on a therapist's advice. This increases the counselor's ethical responsibility to help the client make an autonomous decision rather than one that reflects the therapist's values.

ABORTION COUNSELING AND CONTRACEPTION
COUNSELING

Many observers have commented that the mental health professional counseling the pregnant teenager also has an ethical responsibility to counsel her on avoiding future pregnancies (Brown, 1983; Dornblaser, 1981; Gedan, 1974). Although there may be controversy over the abortion decision itself, there is probably consensus that avoiding pregnancy in the future is desirable for adolescent clients.

Exploring the issue of preventing pregnancy requires examining how the current pregnancy occurred. Many adolescents do not use contraceptives, because they believe they are unlikely to become pregnant, fear their parents' knowledge, or are ignorant about the availability or safety of contraceptives (Zabin & Clark, 1983; Zelnik & Kantner, 1978, 1980). Of course there may be more complex intrapsychic variables involved in the teenager's pregnancy, such as a desire to punish her parents, to create a bond with her boyfriend, or to have the baby as an object of love. The contributing variables may be complex and are clearly the appropriate focus of clinical attention in the postabortion period.

The practical issues relating to contraception are also important in this counseling. In most states minors have relatively free access to contraceptives (Scott, 1984) and the right of persons under 18 to consent to contraceptive services is specifically affirmed by statute, court decision, or attorney general's opinion (Kenney, Forrest, & Torres, 1982). Some states have laws that authorize minors to obtain contraceptives only when referred by such sources as schools, ministers, state agencies, or family planning agencies, or with parental consent (Scott, 1984). A few require parental notice when a minor seeks contraceptives. However, in general most states do not impose significant legal barriers to teenagers' private access to contraceptive services.

A potential serious legal barrier to teenagers' access to contraceptives was a federal regulation proposed by the Department of

Health and Human Services in 1982.[14] This controversial regulation, popularly known as the "squeal rule," required agencies that receive federal funds to notify parents when teenagers obtained contraceptive services. The rule would have affected hundreds of family planning clinics and an estimated 500,000 teenagers receiving prescription contraceptives (Kenney et al., 1982). More than 75% of the states expressed opposition, as did numerous groups including the American Academy of Pediatrics and the American Bar Association (Kenney et al., 1982). The regulation was challenged in two federal circuit courts by the Planned Parenthood Association and has been withdrawn (Scott, 1984).

The clinician working with the pregnant teenager may assist her in examining future contraceptive use. As in the case of abortion, one role of the professional may be to explain how contraceptives may be obtained and any legal regulation or barriers that may exist.

Although issues relating to the sexual behavior of the adolescent may be clinicially complex, the ethical dimensions of contraceptive counseling may be simpler than those of abortion counseling. As Zimring (1982) aptly observed, where the issue is whether a sexually active teenager should use contraceptives, "there is only one preferred public choice." In contrast to the heated controversy regarding teenage abortion, there is strong public support for minors' access to contraceptives (McClosky & Brill, 1983).

THE CLINICIAN AS EVALUATOR

The Supreme Court has endorsed state laws that premise adolescents' access to abortion on a determination that a minor is mature enough to make an independent decision or that the abortion is in her best interests. The expertise of psychologists and other clinicians will likely be sought to assist the decision maker. Some state laws suggest that a rather comprehensive psychological inquiry should be made in deciding whether the minor can make her own

14. *Parental Notification Requirements Applicable to Projects for Family Planning Services*, 42 C.F.R. Part 59, 48 Fed. Reg. 3600 (Jan. 26, 1983).

abortion decision. Missouri, for example, directs the court to receive evidence on the minor's "emotional development, maturity, intellect and understanding."[15] Even where a judicial proceeding is not required by law, mental health input may be sought by the physician who is uncertain of the minor's competency to make the abortion decision. Here the clinical opinion may be decisive in whether an abortion occurs.

The mental health professional in a therapeutic relationship with the teenager may have substantial concern about moving from a treatment role to an evaluative role when called upon, either by the client or by the court, to serve as an expert witness on the adolescent client's maturity. The treating clinician who knows the girl may be in a good position to give an opinion on her capacity to make the abortion decision. Indeed, it may be that through the process of counseling the girl has come to a mature, competent, and informed decision about abortion, and no one could better attest to this than the counselor. However, the prior relationship with the client may create in the therapist a bias that would be absent with a neutral evaluator. Also, the therapeutic relationship may be negatively affected if the therapist concludes that the client lacks the maturity to make the decision.

Other problems arise when the clinician changes roles and becomes an expert witness. The client's expectations about the confidentiality of the therapeutic relationship may be disappointed if the judge decides that, by presenting evidence of her maturity through her therapist, she has waived the psychotherapist/client privilege (Comment, 1980). The judge may then elicit from the clinician communications that the teenage client assumed were part of the confidential therapy relationship. The clinician will wish to explore carefully with the client the implications and risks of any decision to provide expert opinion where the minor seeks abortion. If an abortion counselor associated with a family planning clinic is available to provide information and to assess the minor's competency to provide informed consent, this may be preferable to in-

15. Mo. Rev. Stat. § 188.02862(3) (Supp. 1982).

volving in the judicial process a clinician whose relationship with the minor has a broader therapeutic scope.

The assessment of the minor's capacity to give informed consent is the primary issue on which clinical opinion may be sought. The clinical and legal dimensions of this inquiry have been addressed elsewhere in this volume (see Melton & Pliner). Another legal issue on which mental health expertise may be sought is whether the abortion is in the immature minor's best interests. Even if the teenager is not capable of making her own abortion decision, several laws allow the court to decide that her welfare is best served by abortion without her parents' knowledge or consent (Scott, 1984). If so, the court, under its parens patriae authority to protect the welfare of minors, may order the abortion. Clinical opinion on the potential psychological effects on the girl of abortion or of continued pregnancy may be of some use to the judge in determining whether to authorize the abortion. A number of variables may be significant: the intensity or ambivalence of the girl's desire for an abortion, her capacity to cope with pregnancy, childbirth, and the care of the child, the effect of continued pregnancy on her future plans and expectations, the impact of parental knowledge about the pregnancy, and the potential psychological effects of abortion (cf. Mnookin, 1975).

Clinical opinion on this issue is very problematic. As Zimring (1982) commented, "The decision of whether abortion is in a minor's best interest is a determination made more appropriately by a theologian than by a judge" (or one might add than by a mental health professional). Where professional input is sought, the clinician will do well to adopt a restrained stance on this value-laden issue, withholding opinion on the "ultimate issue" of whether abortion is in the minor's best interests and simply offering clinical observations about the positive and negative effects of each course, given the girl's preferences, her emotional maturity, and her psychological, social, and familial functioning.

Social science research indicates that, contrary to the Supreme Court's opinion in *Matheson*, abortion typically is not substantially more traumatic for adolescents than for adult women (Adler &

Dolcini, this volume; Cates, 1981; Osofsky, Osofsky, Rajan, and Fox, 1971; Pariser, Dixon, & Thatcher, 1978). In individual cases, clinical evaluation may disclose deep ambivalence about the abortion (Friedman, 1973), or religious or moral repugnance that may indicate that abortion may have detrimental psychological effects on a particular girl. However, the common assumption that teenage abortion inherently involves a high risk of damaging psychological effects is not empirically supported.

Ethical problems relating to the clinician's own views about abortion are as significant in the context of a best-interest assessment as they are in the counseling relationship. Mnookin (1983) has pointed out that it is hard to imagine the case in which giving birth to a child against her will would *ever* be in the best interests of the teenager judged too immature to make an abortion decision. Only if the alternative of abortion is viewed as morally abhorrent in general or psychologically damaging in a particular case is the judge or the evaluating clinician likely to reach this conclusion. The risk, as in the counseling situation, is that professional opinion may be influenced by the evaluator's personal bias. A clinician who believes that abortion is the equivalent of murder may foresee many negative consequences for the adolescent based on personal values rather than on neutral clinical observations. Alternatively, some counselors may fail to recognize the client's ambivalence or may overlook external pressure for abortion because they believe that abortion almost always represents the minor's best interests.

CONCLUSION

Abortion counseling of adolescents presents many challenges to the mental health professional. Few clinical issues have such complex legal and ethical dimensions. There are not yet any broadly accepted guidelines that might assist the clinician in the difficult task of counseling the pregnant teenager. It is apparent that the ethical guidelines of different clinical professions must be given careful consideration in this new context. It is also clear that an understanding of the legal framework enhances the clinician's ability to render effective assistance.

REFERENCES

American Academy of Pediatrics, Committee on Adolescence. (1979). Pregnancy and abortion counseling. *Pediatrics, 63,* 920–921.

American Psychological Association. (1981). Ethical principles of psychologists. *American Psychologist, 36,* 633–638.

Bracken, M., Hachamovitch, M., & Grossman, G. (1974). The decision to abort and psychological sequelae. *Journal of Nervous and Mental Disease, 158,* 154–162.

Brown, M. A. (1983). Adolescents and abortion: A theoretical framework for decision making. JOGN *Nursing, 12,* 241–247.

Bush, D. (1983). Fertility-related state laws enacted in 1982. *Family Planning Perspectives, 15,* 111–116.

Bush, S. (1982). Parental notification: A state-created obstacle to a minor woman's right of privacy. *Golden Gate Law Review, 12,* 579–603.

Card, J. J., & Wise, L. (1978). Teenage mothers and teenage fathers: The impact of early childbearing on the parents' personal and professional lives. *Family Planning Perspectives, 10,* 199–205.

Cates, W., Jr. (1981). Abortion for teenagers. In J. E. Hodgson (Ed.), *Abortion and sterilization: Medical and social aspects* (pp. 139–154). London: Academic Press.

Chesler, J., & Davis, S. (1980). Problem pregnancy and abortion counseling with teenagers. *Social Casework, 61,* 173–179.

Comment. (1980). Professional privileges. *Virginia Law Review, 66,* 597–651.

Division of Child, Youth, and Family Services, American Psychological Association. (1982, March). *Ethical principles of psychologists (1981): Suggested additions and revisions.* Proposed revisions endorsed by the executive committee. Washington, DC: Author.

Dornblaser, S. (1981). Pregnancy termination: The abortion decision. *Minnesota Medicine, 64,* 45–47.

Friedman, C.(1973). Making abortion decisions counseling therapeutic. *American Journal of Psychiatry, 130,* 1257–1261.

Furstenburg, F. F., Jr. (1976a). The social consequences of teenage parenthood. *Family Planning Perspectives, 8,* 148–164.

Furstenburg, F. F., Jr. (1976b). *Unplanned parenthood: The social conse-quences of teenage child bearing.* New York: Macmillan.

Garvey, J. (1978). Child, parent, state and the due process clause: An essay on the Supreme Court's recent work. *Southern California Law Review, 51,* 769–822.

Gedan, S. (1974). Abortion counseling with adolescents. *American Journal of Nursing, 74,* 1856–58.

Joffe, C. (1978). What abortion counselors want from their clients. *Social Problems, 26,* 112–121.

Kenney, A., Forrest, J., & Torres, A. (1982). Storm over Washington: The parental notification proposal. *Family Planning Perspectives, 14,* 185–197.

Lidz, C. W., Meisel, A., Zerubavel, E., Carter, M., Sestak, R. M., & Roth, L. H. (1984). *Informed consent: A study of decisionmaking in psychi-atry.* New York: Guilford Press.

Marcus, R. J. (1979). Evaluating abortion counseling. *Dimensions in Health Service, 56*(8), 16–18.

McClosky, H., & Brill, A. (1983). *Dimensions of tolerance: What Americans believe about civil liberties.* New York: Russell Sage Foundation.

Meisel, A. (1979). The "exceptions" to the informed consent doctrine: Striking a balance between competing values in medical decision-mak-ing. *Wisconsin Law Review, 1979,* 413–488.

Melton, G. B. (1983). Minors and privacy: Are legal and psychological concepts compatible? *Nebraska Law Review, 62,* 455–493.

Mnookin, R. H. (1975). Child custody adjudication: Judicial functions in the face of indeterminacy. *Law and Contemporary Problems, 39,* 225–293.

Mnookin, R. H. (1983). *Teenage abortion rights: Policy making by federal courts.* Paper presented at American Psychological Association Conven-tion, Anaheim, California.

Nadelson, C. C. (1974). Abortion counseling: Focus on adolescent preg-nancy. *Pediatrics, 54,* 765–769.

Osofsky, J. D., Osofsky, H. J., Rajan, R., & Fox, M. (1971). Psychologic effects of legal abortion. *Clinical Obstetrics and Gynecology, 14,* 215–234.

Pariser, S., Dixon, K., & Thatcher, K. (1978). The psychiatric abortion consultation. *Journal of Reproductive Medicine, 21,* 171–176.

Scott, E. S. (1984). Adolescents' reproductive rights. In N. D. Reppucci (Ed.), *Children, mental health and the law.* Beverly Hills, CA: Sage.

Legal and Ethical Issues in Counseling Pregnant Adolescents

Torres, A., Forrest, J. D., & Eisman, S. (1980). Telling parents: Clinic policies and adolescents' use of family planning and abortion services. *Family Planning Perspectives, 12*, 284–292.

Trussell, T. (1976). Economic consequences of teenage childbearing. *Family Planning Perspectives, 8*, 184–190.

Wadlington, W. J. (1983). Consent to medical care for minors. In G. Melton, G. Koocher, & M. Saks (Eds.), *Children's competence to consent* (pp. 57–74). New York: Plenum.

Weithorn, L. A., & Campbell, S. B. (1982). The competency of children and adolescents to make informed treatment decisions. *Child Development, 53*, 1589–1598.

Zabin, L. S., & Clark, S. D., Jr. (1983). Institutional factors affecting teenagers' choice and reasons for delay in attending a family planning clinic. *Family Planning Perspectives, 15*, 25–29.

Zelnik, M., & Kantner, J. F. (1978). Contraceptive patterns and premarital pregnancy among women aged fifteen through nineteen in 1976. *Family Planning Perspectives, 10*, 135–142.

Zelnik, M., & Kantner, J. F. (1980). Sexual activity, contraceptive use and pregnancy among metropolitan area teenagers, 1971–1979. *Family Planning Perspectives, 12*, 231–237.

Zimring, F. E. (1982). *The changing legal world of adolescence.* New York: Free Press.

THE AUTHORS

Nancy E. Adler is professor of medical psychology in the Department of Psychiatry and Pediatrics at the University of California, San Francisco, where she is director of the Graduate Program in Health Psychology. She received her Ph.D. in social psychology from Harvard University. Adler's research has focused on social psychological aspects of health behaviors, particularly in reproductive health. Past research has examined psychological sequelae of abortion and psychological issues involved in contraceptive use. Current research is examining adolescent decision making regarding contraceptive use, adolescent risk taking, and the role of psychological variables in obstetrical outcome. Adler is leading a group of researchers at UCSF who are participating in a research network supported by the John D. and Catherine T. MacArthur Foundation on health-promoting and health-damaging behavior.

Peggy Dolcini is pursuing a doctorate in health psychology at the University of California, San Francisco. She holds a master's degree in clinical psychology from San Diego State University and a bachelor's degree from the University of California, Irvine.

Jeanne Marecek is associate professor of psychology at Swarthmore College. She received her Ph.D. in 1973 from Yale University, where she studied social psychology and clinical psychology. Her current interests include gender issues in theories and practice in psychotherapy and the influence of gender-role norms on adolescents' courtship behavior and sexual decision making.

Gary B. Melton is professor of psychology and law and director of the Law/Psychology Program at the University of Nebraska–Lincoln. He received his Ph.D. in clinical-community psychology

The Authors

from Boston University. Melton is president of the Division of Child, Youth, and Family Services of the American Psychological Association and chair of APA's Committee for the Protection of Human Participants in Research. He is an officer of the American Psychology-Law Society and chair of the Courtwatch Committee of the Society for Psychological Study of Social Issues. Melton's primary area of scholarship is child and family policy. He is also interested generally in issues in the application of psychology to the law, and the effects of law upon behavior. Melton is author or editor of 14 books published or in preparation. Among them are *Children's Competence to Consent* and *Child Advocacy: Psychological Issues and Interventions*. In 1985 Melton received the APA's Award for Distinguished Contributions to Psychology in the Public Interest.

Anita J. Pliner is assistant professor of criminal justice at American International College. At the time of her work on this volume, she was a National Institute of Mental Health-supported postdoctoral fellow in the Law/Psychology Program at the University of Nebraska–Lincoln, where she completed a master's degree in psychology. Pliner received her J.D. degree from Syracuse University. Specializing in children's health law and special education law, she has practiced law in Massachusetts.

Nancy Felipe Russo is professor of psychology and director of the Women's Studies Program at Arizona State University. At the time of her contribution to this volume, she was administrative officer for women's programs of the American Psychological Association. A former member of the Subpanel on the Mental Health of Women of the President's Commission on Mental Health, she also serves on the Long-Term Research Committee of the Women's Research and Education Institute of the Congresswoman's Caucus, and she chairs the Mental Health Committee of the Women and Health Roundtable. Author of numerous scientific, professional, and public policy articles, Russo is a Fellow of the American Psychological Association.

The Authors

Elizabeth S. Scott is cofounder and director of the Center for the Study of Children and the Law at the University of Virginia. She received her J.D. degree from the University of Virginia. Her primary area of interest is the application of social science to the development of legal policies relating to children and families. Current research interests include joint custody and the sterilization of mentally retarded persons.

INDEX

Author Index

Author Index

Follingshead, D., 87, 94
Ford, C., 84, 93
Ford, K., 65, 68, 71–72, 97–98, 101, 108, 115
Forrest, J., 130–131, 136
Forrest, J. D., 20, 38, 47, 55–56, 63, 65, 71–72, 117, 137
Forssman, H., 111, 113
Foster, A., 53, 72
Fox, G., 21, 36
Fox, M., 134, 136
Freedman, D., 63, 72
Freeman, E., 78, 93, 110–111, 113
Friedman, C., 134–135
Friedman, H., 16, 36
Furstenberg, F., 20–21, 36, 101–104, 106–107, 114, 121–122, 125, 135

Garvey, J., 118, 136
Gedan, S., 125, 130, 136
Gispert, M., 19, 36
Goldman, A., 11, 35
Goldman, N., 65, 72
Goldsmith, S., 86, 94
Gomes-Schwartz, B., 30, 36
Graves, W., 90, 93
Greenglass, E., 87, 93
Grimes, D., 60, 70
Grisso, T., 18, 36
Grossman, A., 17, 20, 35, 85–87, 92
Grossman, G., 30, 35, 83, 92, 125, 135
Grow, L., 106, 114
Gusdon, J., 88, 93

Hachamovitch, M., 17, 20, 30, 35, 83, 85–87, 92, 125, 135
Hadley, S., 30, 36
Hale, D., 89, 95

Hanson, K., 85, 94
Hardy, J., 64, 72, 102, 114
Harley, H., 87, 94
Harris, T., 101, 113
Hartley, S., 101, 114
Hatcher, S., 75–76, 78–79, 85, 94
Heckel, R., 87, 94
Henderson, G., 69–71
Hendricks, L., 104, 114
Henshaw, S., 47, 59, 71
Henshaw, S. K., 42, 47, 50–51, 53–56, 59, 71
Hirsch, M., 64, 72
Hofferth, S., 101, 114
Holst, E., 16–17, 36, 90, 93
Hook, K., 111, 114

Inazu, J., 21, 36

Janis, I., 75, 94
Joffe, C., 124, 128–129, 136

Kaltreider, N., 75, 86–87, 94
Kamerman, S., 99, 114
Kane, F., 19, 36
Kantner, J., 64, 68, 72, 97–98, 101, 108, 115, 130, 137
Kasl, S., 21, 35
Keith-Spiegel, P., 33, 37
Kenney, A., 47, 130–131, 136
Kinard, E., 107, 114
Kinch, R., 84, 91, 93
Klerman, L., 75, 78–79, 81, 87, 92
Klerman, L. V., 107, 114
Koenig, M., 64, 66, 71
Koocher, G., 18, 27, 37
Kramer, D., 51–52, 71
Kravitz, A., 85, 88–89, 94
Kummer, J., 110, 114
Kurtz, P., 11, 38, 86, 95

Author Index

Author Index

Pliner, A., 57, 109, 119, 133
Poythress, N., 32, 37
Presser, H., 100, 102, 115
Professional Privileges (Comment, *Virginia Law Review*), 132, 135

Rajan, R., 16, 21, 38, 75, 86, 90, 94, 134, 136
Rasmussen, N., 16–17, 36, 81, 90, 93
Rindfuss, R., 91, 94
Rochat, R., 91, 94
Rogers, C., 65, 72
Rosen, R., 20, 38, 80, 95
Roth, L., 123, 136
Rothenberg, P., 21, 38
Rothman, D., 84, 95
Rothstein, A., 89, 95
Rouse, B., 84, 93
Russo, N., 1, 21, 69, 72

Saks, M., 18, 27, 37
Sandler, H., 106, 114
Schaffer, C., 88, 95
Schneider, A., 91, 95
Schrieir, D., 30, 35, 83, 92
Schulz, K., 60, 70
Scott, E., 17, 30, 38, 57, 116–118, 130–131, 133, 136
Selstad, G., 77, 88, 91, 93
Senay, E., 86, 88, 95
Senturia, A., 84, 95
Sestak, R., 123, 136
Shah, F., 63, 72
Shah, F. K., 63, 72
Shapiro, S., 41, 71
Sherrod, K., 106, 114
Simon, N., 84, 95
Slobogin, C., 32, 35, 37
Smetana, J., 78, 95

Smith, E. A., 64, 72
Smith, E. M., 84, 86, 95
Spaulding, J., 84, 95
Spitz, D., 21, 38, 75, 86, 90, 94
Stanley, J., 102, 114
Starfield, B., 41, 71
Stein, Z., 105, 113
Steinhoff, P., 77, 95
Stewart, B., 84, 94
Strupp, H., 30, 36
Suinn, R., 30, 35
Sullivan, E., 47
Sussman, D., 30, 35, 83, 92
Sweet, J., 101, 113

Thatcher, K., 134, 136
Thompson, D., 91, 95
Thornton, A., 63, 72
Thuwe, I., 111, 113
Tietze, C., 42, 47, 49, 51–52, 56–60, 62, 71–72
Tishler, C., 84, 95
Torres, A., 20, 38, 63, 72, 117, 130–131, 136–137
Trussel, T., 121, 137

Unger, I., 90, 92

Vadies, E., 89, 95
Ventura, S., 66–67, 72
Vierling, L., 18, 36
Vietze, P., 106, 114

Wadlington, W., 7–8, 38, 126, 137
Waite, L., 99, 115
Wallerstein, J., 11, 38, 86, 88–89, 95
Wallisch, L., 56, 71
Walter, G., 88, 95
Weinstein, M., 68, 70
Weithorn, L., 8, 18, 39, 123, 137

147

SUBJECT INDEX

Subject Index

Subject Index

152